Strategies For Success

Building An Elementary Music Program

Jane Barbe

Layout and Editing, Brent M. Holl
Editing, Karen F. Holl and Michael R. Nichols
Illustrations, Jamie Lynn-Barbe and Meg Baumgardt
Printed and Distributed by
Beatin' Path Publications, LLC
302 East College Street
Bridgewater, VA 22812

ISBN: 978-0-9832648-0-4

This manual provides supplemental resources for college methods classes, student teachers, and new and veteran teachers alike. College education courses provide the foundation for a successful career as an educator. This book adds essential strategies to apply that knowledge in everyday teaching and addresses each aspect of creating and maintaining a successful music program.

Throughout this book you will find tips on everything from developing lessons, passing out instruments, planning your year, preparing for concerts, to managing your classroom. Since teachers tend to be busy, I present these tips in outline form.

The teaching style in this book relies heavily on process and pacing. Student learning directly relates to making connections between what students already know and what is being taught, like connecting the puzzle pieces or creating links. Pacing is as essential in creating positive classroom management as is stating and modeling expectations clearly.

Supplemental materials can be downloaded at

https://bppub.net/SFS-D-5t6y7S

Full Orff scores for original songs included in this book, a template for a lesson plan book, and many charts, graphs, and images are available to download for use in presentation stations or interactive whiteboards.

— Jane Barbe

Jane Barbe has taught Kindergarten through fifth grade general music and band since 1994. Currently, Jane teaches in the Kyrene School District in Tempe, Arizona. She holds an undergraduate and masters' degree from Ithaca College, as well as Orff Certifications Levels I, II, and III from Arizona State University.

Jane has served as president of the Arizona Chapter of the American Orff-Schulwerk Association. As a clinician, she has presented workshops for state conferences and school districts as well as at the university level. Jane has also served as a mentor teacher since 1998.

Contents

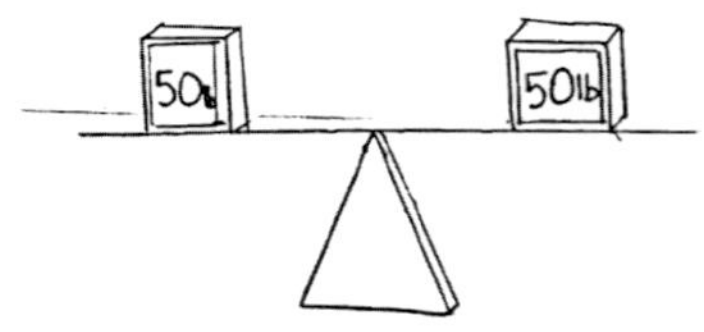

Classroom Management

With so many resources available about classroom management style, the key to success is finding what works best for you and your students.   All classroom management models, however, have common threads.

Effective class management is as important as the concepts being taught. Managing the class with clarity and confidence creates an effective and positive atmosphere in your classroom .

- Establish expectations the first day of class.
- Prevent inappropriate behavior by acknowledging students who follow directions.
- State <u>and</u> model expectations often.
- Pace your lessons efficiently.
- Use cues or key words to get students' attention.
- Use students as models.
- Use proximity.
- Talk to students about behavior.
- Establish consequences.
- Be consistent and follow through.
- Support the classroom teacher's system for rewarding appropriate behavior.
- Express confidence in students' ability to make better choices.
- Give students ownership of their behavior. Ask, *"Should I call home now, or do you think you can make better choices on your own?"*

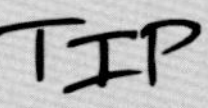

TIP

Before you begin any new activity, state and model what appropriate behavior looks like.

Student behavior depends on the limits you set early in the year. Establish your limits and stick to them. Students will push as far as they can, and too often first-year teachers do not set firm limits for fear of being "mean." Giving a student ten chances before imposing a consequence tells students they have ten chances before something will happen.

To maintain a positive and effective classroom, prevent inappropriate behavior before it happens by acknowledging students doing the right thing. Saying, *"I like how Jane is holding her mallets on her shoulders,"* reinforces Jane for doing the right thing while letting others know what is expected of them.

If you take three minutes or less before each activity to complete the following process, the number of behavioral re-directions will decrease significantly.

> **TIP**
>
> *Be positive. State, "You may stop talking," instead of saying, "You need to stop talking."*

- Before sending students to barred instruments, explain exactly how they move to the instruments and how they wait until ready to play. Say, *"Please walk to instruments slowly and sit quietly with your mallets on your shoulders until I let you know we are ready to play."*
- Show students what that would look like. Actually walk over to the instrument slowly and sit quietly with your mallets on your shoulders.
- Play a short game where you are the student and students are the teacher. Do the above again, but do one step incorrectly (walk slowly to the instruments, but step over one instead of around it or walk to the instrument slowly but play with the mallets right away). On each example, ask a quiet student with a raised hand what was not correct.

> **TIP**
>
> *Silent directions work wonders. When students are not on task, stop talking and start <u>showing</u> them what to do.*

- Send one or two students up to the instruments by themselves and have the rest of students play "detective" to see if they did it correctly.
- When students demonstrate they understand the instructions, send other small groups or send the entire class to the instruments.
- When students are all ready to play, state the next expectation. Say, *"When we stop playing, each of us will stop and immediately put our mallets on our shoulders."* Notice the teacher is included as part of the group.

Pace Your Lessons Efficiently

- With efficient lesson pacing, engaged students have fewer opportunities to make poor choices. Be prepared so you have no gaps in instruction and plan how to keep every student involved throughout the lesson. As a new instrument part is added, teach it to all students instead of teaching it to one group of students. Or have one group of students keep the beat or be "detectives" and offer observations about the other groups' progress or performance.

> **TIP**
>
> *When students are giving feedback to the class, have them use words like, "I saw three students playing the drum correctly," rather than using student names.*

The music room can be a loud environment, especially when classroom instruments are used. Use a cue, an essential tool, to tell students when to stop moving and/or playing.

- Use a conductor's cut off.
- State, *"Freeze and look at me,"* or *"Freeze and take a seat."*
- Call out the school's name and have students freeze and call out the mascot name in response.
- Use a predetermined rhythm on the drum.

I can tell students to put down their mallets five times, but some may not comply. If I state, *"I like how Jane has her mallets down,"* students all immediately follow.

Use Students as Models

Student modeling is especially useful when some students are unsuccessful in what you are having them do. Asking another student to demonstrate is more effective than modeling it yourself.

Use Proximity

Always move around the room while teaching. When cues and stating expectations are not working, look directly at, stand or sit next to the student in question, or non-verbally show them what to do.

Talk to Students (and Parents) About Behavior

Often, something occurring outside the classroom can affect a student's performance and behavior in class. When it becomes necessary to talk to an individual student about their inappropriate behavior, ask if something is bothering them. If so, offer a solution to help the student return to the class activity. Say, *"We are going to play instruments. I know you can be a good listener and follow directions. If I give you a couple of minutes to sit out and cool down, do you think you would be ready to listen when we go to the instruments? If they respond with a "no," say, "I trust you to know how much time you will need. Raise your hand when you are ready."*

If a simple intervention doesn't work, ask the student if they feel you should call home now or whether they think they can correct their behavior. Typically students choose to correct their own behavior; therefore, state the number of classes they have to correct their behavior before you contact parents. Make sure to thank the student and reassure them you know they have the ability to change. Communicate with students and parents earlier rather than later.

> **TIP**
>
> *Prevent inappropriate behavior before it happens by acknowledging students who are doing the right thing. Say, "I like how Jane is holding her mallet on her shoulders."*

- Assure parents they know their child best and ask for more information about the student to help you understand them better.
- Create the sense of a team between the student, teacher, and parents.
- Help the student succeed by creating a plan with the student and/or parents. Ask, *"Would it help you if I hold up a finger when you are calling out? No one will know the signal but the two of us."*
- Talk to the classroom teacher about what has worked for that particular student.

Establish Consequences

Consequences should be considered in terms of school policies and the regular teacher's classroom management system. You should only choose a consequence you can be enforce.

- Have the student move to another space.
- Take their instrument for the moment or for the rest of class.
- Replace their instrument with a silent alternative (box or pencil), or have the student use their fingers instead of mallets. Playing privileges can be earned back with good behavior.
- Use a time-out.
- Take away recess. (If you take away recess, avoid imposing on the classroom teacher; have the student come to your room to serve the time unless your school has an established detention program.)

Support the Classroom Teacher's System

Classroom teachers typically have a system to account for student behavior throughout the day. They often have a behavior level chart represented by symbols or colored cards to record student behavior. This sample uses colored cards.

- Start every student at a green card.
- Allow each student two redirections before they move their color to yellow and then red.
- At the end of the day, students on yellow receive a note home to their parents.
- Students on red receive a phone call home and loss of recess the next day.
- When the class arrives, find out which students are already on yellow or red.
- When the classroom teacher picks up the students, indicate who received warnings.

Prevent "Follow the Leader"

In elementary school, if one student asks to get a drink or go to the bathroom, everyone else will, too! Let one student go to the bathroom at a time. Also ask if it is an emergency because most teachers give students bathroom breaks right before or after my class. If more than a few ask to be excused, let the teacher know.

TIP

For more information on classroom management, read **Teaching With Love and Logic: Taking Control of the Classroom** *(Funk and Fay). Students are taught to understand their behavior is their responsibility, lessening the need for consequences.*

Sequencing Concepts Throughout the Year

Some districts provide specific curriculums and supplemental resources with lessons pre-written and scheduled for certain weeks of the year while other districts just have a general list of concepts to be taught. Sequence the year depending on the needs of students and when the concerts occur. Although all concepts are experienced continuously and spiral throughout the year, designate certain months or quarters to specifically isolate and focus on each key concept. For example, in the second quarter of second grade, the notated half note will be taught. Before the second quarter, students will have experienced playing, moving, and reading half note notation. After teaching the half note, students will continue to experience half notes while isolating other concepts.

Concepts for the Year

Beat	**Tempo**
Vocal Technique	**Form**
Timbre	**Melody**
Instrument Technique	**Meter**
Rhythm	**Harmony**
Dynamics	

1st Quarter

- Vocal technique (use correct singing voice and match pitch)
- Timbre (identify classroom instruments by family, name, and sound)
- Instrument technique (learn correct techniques for playing recorder, barred instruments, small percussion, and drums)
- Beat (keep the beat in two levels of the body [stomp and clap] or use beat passing games) Here is an example:

I Like Food

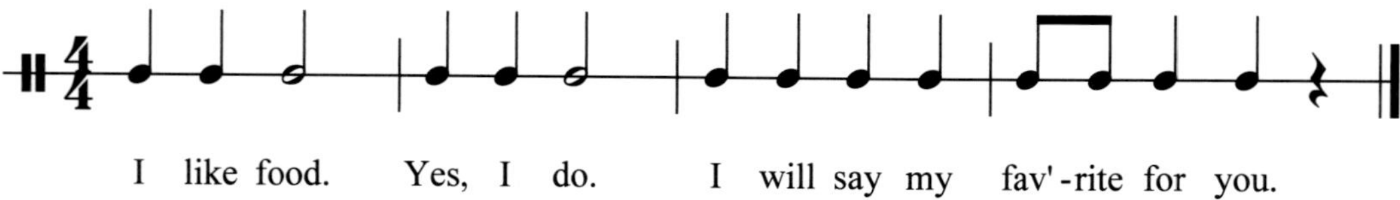

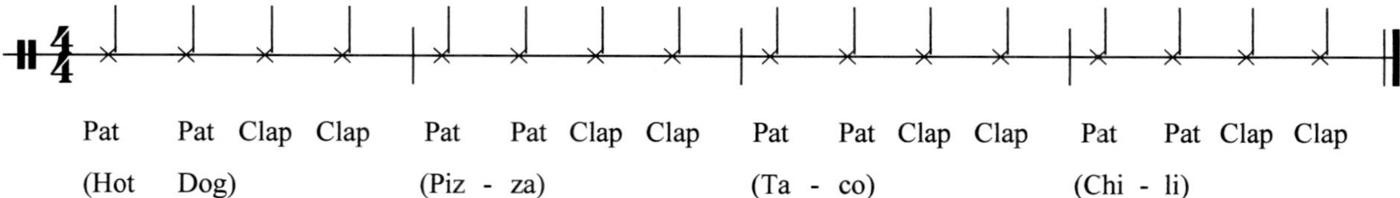

Process
- Establish a body percussion pattern (Pat, Pat, Clap, Clap) to keep the beat.
- Teach the rhythm and lyrics of the rhyme.
- Have students perform rhyme with the body percussion pattern.
- Teach the response section.
- Have students go around the circle in order stating a food they enjoy on the Pat part of the body percussion pattern.
- When the students are proficient saying their word on time, you may choose to make it a game with outs. Any student who repeats the same food or misses saying their food on the correct beats is out.

Form
- The class begins the body percussion pattern which continues throughout the game until someone is out or the class in no longer accurately representing the beat.
- The teacher cues the entire class to say the rhyme.
- The teacher immediately states the first response on the first Pat, Pat pattern after the rhyme is completed followed by each student around the circle.

2nd Quarter
- Rhythm (identify and play half note)
- Dynamics (identify and play *crescendo, decrescendo, mezzo piano, piano, mezzo forte, forte*)
- Form (identify and play introduction and coda; introduce rondo)

3rd Quarter
- Meter (play beat games such as *I Like Food*)
- Melody (sing mi, re, do; review of sol, la)

4th Quarter
- Tempo (identify and play accelerando and ritardando)
- Harmony (play partner songs and rounds)

You can find lessons and activities in district-adopted texts, in purchased lesson books, and from workshops. As you progress through the year, keep a list of successful activities for every concept and grade level. This list will come in handy for planning subsequent years and can be kept on the computer for simple modification.

Plan Book Organization:
Keeping Track of Each Class

Plan books accommodating the structure of special area classes are hard to find. A plan book devised of weekly planning charts reflecting a specials type schedule, however, keeps track not only of the skills in each grade level curriculum, but also the progress of each individual class.

- Each class works at a different pace depending on student ability, behavior, and events such as field days, assemblies, and holidays.
- Use a square per class in a weekly planning chart to record class-specific information. The chart can be quickly referenced between classes. Position it on a wall or bulletin board and make notes after class.
- Using one square for each class session enables changes to be made easily without having a messy permanent plan book. Make changes in pencil during the week as necessary.

On the next page, you will find a sample of my plan book which includes:
- class times and teachers' names (teacher's name replaces 2nd Grade A)
- the first class of the week italicized and underlined
- the second class of the week not italicized or underlined
- the behavior plan for each classroom teacher marked under the teacher's name (Keys, TT, Compliments)
    - » Keys: The teacher gives students three keys at the beginning of each day. If a student misbehaves, the teacher removes a key. Each key taken away has a specific, pre-set consequence.
    - » TT: Terrific Time is a classroom teacher-led reward activity occurring every Friday afternoon. Students who earn the privilege participate in Terrific Time.
    - » Compliments: Compliments are class rewards for receiving compliments from the music, art, or physical education teachers for respectful behavior. When the students receive a specific number of compliments, the class receives a pre-set award.

To create the yearly plan book, copy one chart for each week of the school year, add the date to each page, and place them in a three-ring binder. Each week, take out the one for the coming week, fill it out, and position it where you can easily access it for the week. Near the end of each week, fill out the next week's chart and place the old one back in the notebook. At the end of the year, bind them together for later reference. (You can find a blank planning page template in the Supplemental Materials.)

<table>
<tr><th colspan="6">Week of September 10</th></tr>
<tr><td></td><th>Monday</th><th>Tuesday</th><th>Wednesday</th><th>Thursday</th><th>Friday</th></tr>
<tr><td>8:30-9:00</td><td>2nd Grade A
Keys</td><td>2nd Grade B
Keys</td><td>2nd Grade A
Keys</td><td>2nd Grade B
Keys</td><td>5th Grade A
Keys</td></tr>
<tr><td>9:05-9:35</td><td>2nd Grade C
Keys</td><td>2nd Grade D
Keys</td><td>5th Grade C
TT</td><td>2nd Grade C
Keys</td><td>(9:10-9:40)
2nd Grade
Keys</td></tr>
<tr><td>9:40-10:10</td><td>5th Grade A
Compliments</td><td>5th Grade B
Compliments</td><td>5th Grade D
TT</td><td>5th Grade B
TT</td><td>5th Grade D
TT</td></tr>
<tr><td>10:15-10:45</td><td>3rd Grade A
TT</td><td>3rd Grade B
TT</td><td>3rd Grade A</td><td>5th Grade C
TT</td><td>3rd Grade B</td></tr>
<tr><td>11:00-11:30</td><td>4th Grade A
Compliments</td><td>4th Grade A
TT</td><td>2nd Grade E
Keys</td><td>4th Grade B
Keys</td><td>2nd Grade E
TT</td></tr>
<tr><td>11:30-12:00
Planning
12:00-12:40
Lunch</td><td></td><td></td><td></td><td></td><td></td></tr>
<tr><td>12:45-1:15</td><td>4th Grade B</td><td>4th-Grade C
Keys</td><td>(12:30-1:00)
4th Grade D
Compliments</td><td>4th Grade C
Keys</td><td>4th Grade D</td></tr>
<tr><td>1:20-1:50</td><td>3rd Grade C</td><td>3rd Grade D</td><td>District Early Release Day</td><td>3rd Grade C</td><td>3rd Grade D</td></tr>
<tr><td>1:55-2:25</td><td>3rd Grade E</td><td>1st Grade A</td><td></td><td>3rd Grade E</td><td>1st Grade A</td></tr>
<tr><td>2:30-3:00</td><td>1st Grade B</td><td>1st Grade C</td><td></td><td>1st Grade B</td><td>1st Grade C</td></tr>
</table>

Lesson Plan for the First Day of School

The first day of school has two immediate objectives: engaging students in stimulating learning activities while establishing procedures and expectations. This sample lesson process incorporates a mixer as the musical activity and covers teaching behavioral expectations, entry and exit procedures, and aural and physical cues.

Enter the Room

- Meet students at the door; have music with a strong beat playing inside your classroom.
- Silently begin a beat-keeping motion for students to copy.
- Have students follow you into a circle and change your motions on each phrase so they know to watch and follow.
    - » Tap shoulders or chest
    - » Pat legs (patschen)
    - » Stomp
    - » Snap
    - » Swish hands (rub them together back and forth)
    - » Jump
    - » Jumping Jacks (if students are able to do them on the beat)

Kindergartners start with these motions while first graders progress to performing them with alternate hands or feet. Older grades can perform sequences of motions: pat, clap; pat, clap, snap; or stomp, pat, clap, snap.

Establish Behavior Cues

As soon as the music ends, establish the first cue for the year. The type of cue does not matter as much as keeping it consistent. Say, *"Freeze and look at me,"* or *"Freeze and take a seat."* State this cue and explain each time it is heard, students are expected to freeze and look at you or sit down.

- As soon as the students have responded with the cue to freeze and sit, begin silently modeling the motions of the mixer activity. Students echo the motions (stomp, clap, rest, rest).

14

Modern Mixer

Jane Barbe

B Section

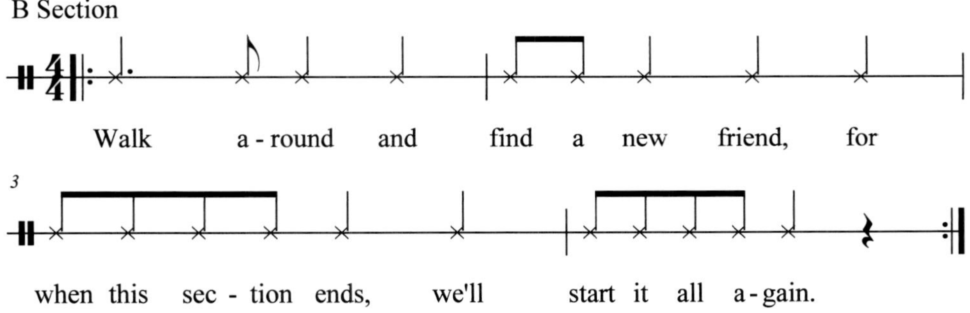

- Partner = Tap hands with partner as in a hand jive.
- Be creative with these movements. Change them each time students meet a new friend or have the movements be cumulative depending on the level of students.
- Form = AB continually repeated until the teacher decides to end the song by adding a ritardando to the end of the A Section.

Process

- Silent directions work to focus students' attention. Without giving directions verbally, the teacher points to self, performs a motion, and points to students to repeat the motion.
- Typically motions are learned by phrase. When students proficiently perform the first motion, teach the remainder by adding one at a time. Ask, *"Please watch what I am doing. Tell me what I am adding and where I add it."*
- Teach the melody by connecting it to the motion for each phrase. Use echoing solfege patterns and/or echoing melodic phrases with the lyrics.
- Have students choose one partner to perform the motions while simultaneously singing the song.
- Give the students cue to freeze and sit.

- Explain rules, behavioral expectations, and consequences.
- When finished, return to the song, and teach the section in which they will move to a new partner.
- As a final step, perform the entire song as a mixer.
- If the lesson is paced appropriately, the final performance of the mixer will occur in the last few minutes of class, immediately followed by the line up procedure.

Learn to Line Up

- Show and tell students how to line up at the door. The classroom teacher may have a specific line order established (number order or alphabetical order). Use the same procedure after receiving this information from the classroom teacher in advance.
- Use a game, such as *The Quiet Game* or *Twenty Questions,* to keep students quiet and focused until the teacher arrives. When in line, deliver a reflective question about what was done during class or about a concept introduced as closure to the lesson.

The Quiet Game
- *Say, "We are going to line up and play the quiet game on the count of 3." Say, "1, 2, 3, silence" or, "1, 2, 3, freeze."*
- Find a quiet student, facing forward with their arms by their sides. He/she leaves the line to choose the next person, and the game continues until the teacher arrives.

Twenty Questions
- Ask the children questions about the lesson just completed. Ask about simple concepts or directions to the games students are supposed to remember.
- Reinforce classroom procedures by letting students know only quiet students with raised hands will be chosen.

Primary

- ***Singing Games Children Love Volume 1*** (Gagne)
    - » *Rig a Jig Jig* (Add a partner changing component to this game.)
    - » *Sailor Went to Sea Sea Sea*
    - » *Bow Wow Wow*
- ***Jump Jim Joe: Great Singing Games for Children*** (Amidon)
    - » *Jump Jim Joe*
- ***Down in the Valley: More Great Singing Games for Children*** (Amidon)
    - » *Down in the Valley*

Intermediate

- ***Down in the Valley: More Great Singing Games for Children*** (Amidon)
    - » *Four White Horses*
    - » *Step It Down*
- ***120 Singing Games for Elementary Schools*** (Brummitt)
    - » *Four White Horses*
    - » *Long Legged Sailor*
    - » *I've Got Rhythm* (Create transition music for students to find new partners.)
- ***Game Plan Grade 3*** (Kriske and DeLelles)
    - » *Up the Ladder (Name Game)*
- ***Singing Games Children Love Volume 1*** (Gagne)
    - » *John Kanakanaka*

The Second, Third, and Fourth Lessons of the Year

Use the second, third, and fourth lessons to capture student excitement through instrument activities and beat competency games. These lessons also reinforce instrument playing techniques.

During this lesson students work musically as a group with instruments they enjoy such as drums and/or Boomwhackers®. Pass out unpitched instruments and teach students how to play them correctly.

Kindergarten
- Drums
  - » *Stop and Go* (Jenkins), but modified to say, *"I'm gonna play and play and play and stop."*
- Boomwhackers®
  - » *Hickory Dickory Dock* from ***Fun With Boomwhackers®*** (Judah-Lauder)

1st Grade
- Drums
  - » *I Think Music's Neat* from ***Game Plan Grade 1*** (Kriske and DeLelles)
  - » Rhyme: 2, 4, 6, 8, Meet Me at the Garden Gate, If I'm Late, Please Don't Wait, 2, 4, 6, 8. Students drum on the numbers and walk the beat on the words.
- Boomwhackers®
  - » *Happy and You Know It* from ***Fun With Boomwhackers®*** (Judah-Lauder)

2nd Grade
- Drums
  - » *Drum Beat* from ***Hand Drums on the Move*** (Judah-Lauder)
- Boomwhackers®
  - » *Diddle Diddle Dumpling* from ***Fun With Boomwhackers®*** (Judah-Lauder)

3rd Grade
- Drums
  - » *Talk to Me* from ***Game Plan Grade 3*** (Kriske and DeLelles)

4th Grade
- Drums
- Boomwhackers®

TIP

If you want students to try each type of instrument or you do not have an instrument for each child, use an interlude to have students rotate. Use a chant to start their rotation.

Instruments down on the floor,
Now we're ready to play some more.

» *Getting Around* from ***Fun With Boomwhackers*** (Judah-Lauder)

5th Grade

- Drums
  - » *As I Was Sitting in My Chair* from ***Conga Town*** (Solomon)
- Boomwhackers®
  - » *Flip and Hit or Take Your Pick* from ***Fun With Boomwhackers*** (Judah-Lauder)

Third Lesson of the Year

Continue to build excitement while reviewing Orff instrument technique and giving students an opportunity to play each of the instruments through a rotation activity. The activities for first, second, and third grades each have the Orff instruments set in a pentatonic scale allowing students to play any bars they choose on the repetitive words in songs or rhymes. Having no half steps, pentatonic scales allow students to create and improvise simultaneously with beautiful sound.

In the fourth and fifth grade activities, students play melodic ostinatos (repetitive patterns) which combine to create harmony. Pieces like these are good for the first weeks of school because they are simple enough to learn in one class period and give students the rich, full sound of a large ensemble.

1st Grade

- Rhyme: Students play a simple chord bordun on the "pop's."

Popcorn

Pop, pop, pop
Says the popcorn in the pan.
Pop, pop, pop
You may catch me if you can.
Pop, pop, pop
As they scamper across the heat.
Pop, pop, pop
They are very good to eat!
Pop, pop, pop

Goes the popcorn in the pan.
Pop, pop, pop
Try to catch me if you can.
Pop, pop, pop
Go my kernels bright and yellow.
Pop, pop, pop
I'm a happy little fellow.
Pop, pop, pop, pop, pop, pop, pop

2nd Grade
- ◆ *Go Go Go* from **Game Plan Grade 3** (Kriske and DeLelles)
- ◆ *Fuzzy Wuzzy* from **Game Plan Grade 3** (Kriske and DeLelles)

4th Grade
- ◆ *2, 3* from **Hot Marimba** (Hampton)

5th Grade
- ◆ *Mbira Jam* from **Hot Marimba** (Hampton)

Fourth Lesson of the Year

This lesson reinforces steady beat and teamwork. Sitting in a circle, students pass a bean bag to the beat or pass the beat with their hands.

Banana Split

Jane Barbe

Formation: Students sit in a circle close enough their knees almost touch.

Set-Up

- ◆ Students lift right hands in the air and place left hands, palm up, on their left knees.
- ◆ Students bring right hands down, palm up, on top of their neighbor's left.
- ◆ The first student to begin passing the beat lifts their right hand and moves it over to tap the hand of their neighbor to the left.
- ◆ Ensure the set up is correct by having students pass the beat once around the circle.

Game Directions

- Establish the introduction as ♩ ♩ ♫♩.
- Designate one student to begin passing the beat on the first beat of the song.
- Students continue passing the beat until the last word of the song.
- The student tapped on the last word, Splat, is out and goes to play the beat on an unpitched instrument, an accompaniment on Orff instruments, or to sit behind a student still in the game.

Extensions

- Direction changes add complexity in a game where an object is passed. Before the game begins, the teacher designates a particular word in the song to become the direction-changing point. Another word may also be designated to return the object to the original direction.

Note: The game can be played with or without accompaniment.

Other Beat Passing Games
2nd Grade
- *Acca Bacca* from **Game Plan Grade 1** (Kriske and DeLelles)

3rd Grade
- *Stella Ella Olla* from **120 Singing Games and Dances for Elementary Schools** (Brummitt)

4th Grade
- *Down By the Banks* from **Game Plan Grade 1** (Kriske and DeLelles)

5th Grade
- *Down Down Baby, Down By the Roller Coaster.*

After these lessons, focus on specific concepts as outlined in **Sequencing Your Year**.

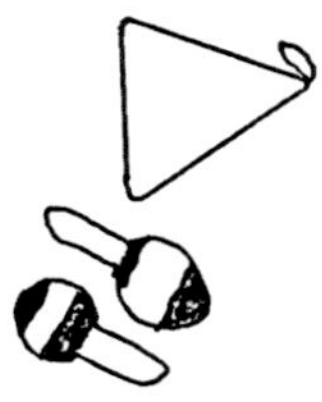

How to Hand Out Instruments Efficiently

- Show students the instrument and demonstrate proper playing technique.
- Explain how to pass instruments around the circle.
    - » Hand instruments, one at a time, to a chosen student who passes each instrument around the circle to his/her right.
    - » Students in the circle continue to pass the instrument from person to person until it reaches the last one in the circle.
    - » As each student receives an instrument, he/she places it on the floor, alerting the next person to do the same with his/her instrument. This process continues until all students have received and placed their instruments.
- Explain what students do when they get their instruments.
    - » Say, *"Instruments down, hands in lap."* On this cue, students gently place the instrument on the floor and put their hands in their lap.
    - » State a possible consequence positively. Say, *"You will be able to keep your instrument as long as you follow the cue."*

When students uses this process, you can pass out instruments quickly and efficiently.

- Show students which instruments they will play.
- Explain how they move to the instruments, using options like these.
    - » Call students by shirt color, birthday, or type of shoes and *direct them to the instruments you would like them to play.*
    - » Call students by shirt color, birthday, or type of shoes and *let them pick the instrument they would like to play.*
    - » Hand students a card with the name of the instrument they

will play and have students find it.

> » Line students up single file and ferry them to the instruments.

- Explain how students wait at the instruments until time to play.

> » Ask students to stand with hands behind their back (not touching mallets or instruments).

> » Ask students waiting to be sent to an instrument to be "detectives" who watch for people following directions.

- If students need to set up instruments in a certain scale, show them the proper way to take off the bars. They should hold the bar with two hands, one on the top and one on the bottom, lifting straight up to prevent the pegs from being bent and broken.

- Now have students play the instruments, at first with finger tips only, no mallets. This ensures they play the part correctly and makes having the mallets a reward for doing a great job.

Logical Sequencing, Connections, and Pacing

Student learning directly relates to the teacher's ability to sequence the lesson by not only linking each step to the next, but also building on previous knowledge. This section contains two lesson plans written out word for word where you see these links created through open-ended questions.

> **Concepts: Iconic half-note recognition; accelerando, dynamics.**
> **Example:** *In the Hall of the Mountain King* by Edvard Grieg

Note: Options for saying rhythms include attaching students names, foods, or animal names to their respective rhythms. In the example I use *ta* for quarter notes, *ta-a* for two tied quarter notes, *ti-ti* for eighth notes, and *to-oe* for the written half notes.

- Students enter the room keeping the beat to a recording of *In the Hall of the Mountain King* from the *Peer Gynt Suite* by Edvard Grieg. The teacher stops the recording before the accelerando begins.
- When students are in a circle and have experienced keeping the beat to this piece in several places on their body, the teacher leads the following discussion.

TEACHER: Does anyone remember the new rhythm we learned last class with the *Baa Baa Black Sheep* game?

STUDENT: *Ta-a.*

TEACHER: Yes, the *ta-a.* How did the *ta-a* look different than just a *ta*?

STUDENT: The *ta-a* has two *ta's* which have a smiley face thing under them.

TEACHER: Yes, the *ta's* with the smiley face under them. Correct. Does anyone know what the smiley face thing is called?

STUDENT: A tie.

TEACHER: Yes, right, a tie. How many beats is a *ta*?

STUDENT: One.

TEACHER: One, yes. So, if two *ta's* are tied together, how many beats would that equal?

STUDENT: Two beats. Can someone find a *ta-a* on the board? (The teacher points to the chart of *In the Hall of the Mountain King* and allows several students to come to the board until the *ta-a* has been found.)

TEACHER: Today our goal is to learn what the *ta-a* rhythm really looks like in music. (The teacher reads aloud and points to the objective written on the board.)

- The class reads the rhythmic pattern together with rhythm syllables (*ti-ti ta*).
- Pass out rhythm sticks .
- Have students read the rhythmic pattern.
    - » Say.
    - » Say and play.
    - » Whisper and play.
    - » Use Silent Lips and play. (Silent Lips are like lip syncing. Students silently say the pattern.)

TEACHER: When you want to say you have two pencils, do you just write "pencil pencil" like we did with the *ta-a*'s?

STUDENT: No.

TEACHER: What do you do?

STUDENT: You add an "s" to the end.

TEACHER: So when you add the "s" to create the word "pencils," does it look exactly the same as the word "pencil"?

STUDENT: No.

TEACHER: Does it look totally different?

STUDENT: No, just a little different…there's an "s" on the end.

TEACHER: In music, when we want to say we have more than one beat, we also have to make our notes look a little different. Look at this note. h What is different?

STUDENT: There is no filling.

STUDENT: It's not filled in.

TEACHER: The note has no filling, or it's not filled in. I like how you explained that. We call this a half note and to play it we say *to-oe*. This is the way a half note is written. Why do you think I wrote this note as two *ta*'s tied together before?

STUDENT: To show us it equaled two beats just like two *ta*'s tied together.

- Have students play and say the pattern with the correct half note notation and the *to-oe* sound.
- Pass the rhythm sticks back in.
- Have students read the pattern with Silent Lips, but vocalize <u>only</u> the *ta*'s. Add a patsch (pat) to the *ta*'s.
- Have students read the pattern with Silent Lips, vocalizing the *ta*'s and the *to-oe*. Add a clap and hold for the *to-oe*.
- Add the *ti-ti*'s in the feet with stomps.
- After successfully performing the piece with body percussion, have students sit and listen to the piece, ***In the Hall of the Mountain King***, and figure out why this particular piece is the lesson. (The rhythm pattern on the board matches the one in the song).

TEACHER: Once, a long time ago, more than 150 years ago in fact, a man named Edvard Grieg was born in a country called Norway. He loved to play the piano. When he got older, his friend who wrote plays came to him and asked him to write the music for his play based on the Norwegian folk tale, *"Peer Gynt."* Have you ever been to a movie? Have you ever noticed the music in the background? Well, this is what Edvard Grieg was writing for his friend's play. In the play, Peer Gynt, a daydreamer who lives at home with his mom, often gets himself into trouble. One day he was chased by trolls. Our music today is the music Mr. Grieg wrote for the troll chase.

- Students read the notation from the chart introduced at the beginning of the lesson with Silent Lips along with the song, performing their body percussion. (The teacher again stops the piece before the accelerando.)

Stop here if class time is finished; otherwise continue with the lesson.

- After students successfully perform the body percussion with the piece up to the accelerando, have students repeat the performance letting the recording play to the end <u>without</u> informing them of the changes which will occur.

TEACHER: What happened in the song?
STUDENT: It got faster. It had an accelerando.
STUDENT: It got louder, a crescendo.
TEACHER: Why would Edvard Grieg have the music get faster and louder?
STUDENT: Because it is a chase scene. It makes it exciting.
STUDENT: It makes it scary.
TEACHER: Yes, it does all of those things. Do you think we could perform the pattern all the way to the end?
STUDENTS: Yes.
STUDENT: I don't know.
TEACHER: I think we can. Here is a clue which might help us. Sometimes when the music goes faster, we just go wild and forget about the pattern, but if we do our best on the 8th notes and make sure we get all of the *ta's,* I think we can make it to the end accurately.

- Students usually perform the piece once more for practice and once for the final performance.
- At the end of the lesson, the teacher asks these questions.

TEACHER: What was the name of the piece we performed today?
STUDENT: *In the Hall of the Mountain King.*
TEACHER: Why did the composer, Edvard Grieg, add an accelerando and a crescendo?
STUDENT: Because the trolls were chasing Peer Gynt.

TEACHER: We learned a new rhythm today. Does anyone remember what it was called?
STUDENT: A half note but we used the word *to-oe*.
TEACHER: Correct. How will we tell the difference between a *ta* and a *to-oe*?
STUDENT: The *to-oe* is not filled in.
TEACHER: Yes, it is not filled in. When it has a stem like a *ta*, but is not filled in, how many beats is the note?
STUDENT: Two.
TEACHER: So, if we were to complete this number sentence what would the sum be?

$$2 + 1 + 2 = 5$$

Concept: AB Form
Example: *La Raspa*

Teacher leads students into the room to a recording of *La Raspa* and directs them into a circle. A chart showing the melodic pattern written with maracas instead of notes is displayed at the front of the room. The teacher keeps the beat in different places on the body with students copying the teacher. The teacher changes where he/she keeps the beat at the end of each phrase. At the end of the song, bow on the last two beats. Options for keeping the beat are pat, clap, stomp, jump, hop on one foot, jump in a circle, jumping jacks, shrug shoulders, bounce, or blink eyes.

TEACHER: We just listened to a very famous song. Today, we are going to figure out what country it is from and learn part of a dance which goes with this song. Let's listen to the song again, and this time you have a job. Your job is to think in your mind about what country you think it is from.

- The teacher models good listening for students by asking some questions before listening again.

TEACHER: If I am listening, what will I look like?
STUDENTS: Sitting still. Not talking. Hands to ourselves.
TEACHER: Yes, correct. If I figure out the answer, should I yell it out right in the middle of the song?
STUDENTS: No.
TEACHER: What should I do?
STUDENTS: Wait until the end of the song?
TEACHER: Then can I yell out the answer?
STUDENT: No, you raise your hand and wait.
TEACHER: That's a great idea. Let's listen and figure out what country this song is from.

- After the song finishes, choose a student waiting quietly with a raised hand.

TEACHER: Yes, this song is from Mexico. It is called La Raspa. Let's say that together. Does anyone
           know an instrument from Mexico we have in this room?
STUDENT: A maraca.
TEACHER: Yes, a maraca. Let's look up at the board. Does anyone see a maraca?
STUDENT: Yes, there are many. (Refer to the melodic pattern chart on display.)

- Teach the melody of the A Section by referring to the chart board and teaching the English
  words for that part.
- When they can sing the melody, ask students to stand when that melody is heard. They should
  remain seated or return to the seated position when the melody is not heard. Play the recording.
  When they sit for the first time, I stop the music right away.

TEACHER: Why did everyone sit down?
STUDENTS: The music stopped.
TEACHER: Maybe, but I still heard the music coming from the speakers.
STUDENTS: The melody went away.
TEACHER: Correct. I wonder how many times we will hear that part during the song? Let's see.

- Play the entire song having students sit and stand when appropriate. (Don't help them with
  activities like this if the point is to assess if they can hear the changes in the music.)

TEACHER: Wow, you are all doing such a great job listening for that part of the music. We should
           name that part. Usually we start at the beginning of the alphabet. What do you think it
           should be called?
STUDENT: A. That is a very famous song.
TEACHER: Correct. What do we call the part where we sat down? Can we call it A, too?
STUDENT: No.
TEACHER: Why not?
STUDENT: Because it isn't the same.
TEACHER: So, if it is not the same it must be….?
STUDENTS: Different.
TEACHER: Ok, so what should we call it?
STUDENTS: B.

- If students are successful, teach the dance moves for part A and have students perform with
  the recording, while continuing to sit when the A Section goes away.

TEACHER: I will see if everyone is still in their places in the circle. We need to look like a donut, not a
           wet, wiggly noodle.

TEACHER: I am impressed. Everyone stayed in their spots in the circle and remembered to listen so they only did the hop step when they heard the A Section. Today we learned the A part of the dance. Next class we will learn the B part which is fun because you get to do it with a friend. Where was our song from today? (Mexico.) What did we call the part of the music we danced to today? (A.)

Next Class Session

TEACHER: Does anyone remember where our dance from last class was from?
STUDENTS: Mexico.
TEACHER: What did we do with our bodies when we were not dancing?
STUDENTS: We sat.
TEACHER: Why did we sit?
STUDENT: Because the music was different.
TEACHER: Oh, yes, right. Does anyone remember what we called that part of the music which was different from our (say the words of the song) dancing part?
STUDENT: B.
TEACHER: Today we are going to finish this dance by learning what to do during the B Section.

- Have students choose partners. Arrange the partner sets in two concentric circles facing their partner. (Partner A should be on the outside circle and Partner B on the inside circle.)
- Demonstrate the B Section of the dance.
- Have students perform the B Section dance only with every B Section on the recording.
- Put the entire piece together.
- Practice.
- Perform for the teacher.

TEACHER: Today we finished our *La Raspa* dance. What kind of move did we do during the A Section? What did we do during the B Section? Why couldn't we have done the hops during the whole song? (Use other appropriate questions to reinforce learning.)

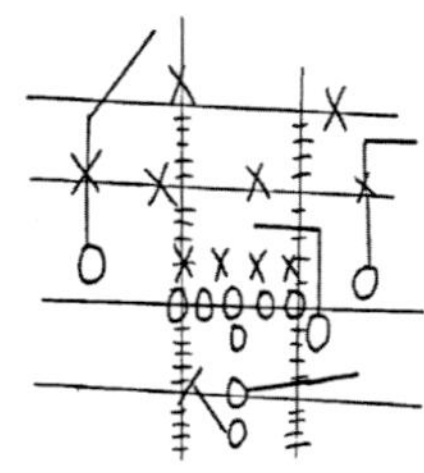

Strategies for Teaching Elements of Music

Using movement powerfully allows students to feel the rhythm.

- Assign movements to particular rhythms (quarter notes = walk, half notes = sway, and eighth notes = tiptoe). The teacher plays one rhythm on a designated instrument (quarter notes on a drum). Students move with the rhythm of the drum until another rhythm is introduced on a different instrument. Add as many rhythms and instruments as students can handle. Play a game where you switch at the end of each phrase, but unexpectedly change the pattern. Challenge more advanced students to perform two rhythms simultaneously with different body parts (walk the beat in the feet while clapping eighth notes).

- Have students perform the beat in their feet. When an instrument cue is heard, they begin clapping eighth notes. When another instrument cue is heard, they switch to patting sixteenth notes.

- In a circle, have students walk forward eight beats into the middle of the circle while the teacher claps a four-beat rhythmic pattern. The students echo clap the teacher's rhythmic pattern while walking the beat backwards out of the circle.

- Have a certain part of the room designated for walking the beat. Place a string on the floor to designate another area as a clapping place for eighth notes and another area for patting sixteenth notes (Fig. 1). Students may switch areas whenever they feel ready or may straddle two areas and perform two movements/rhythms simultaneously. The teacher should always give the beat as a reference on an instrument such as a drum.

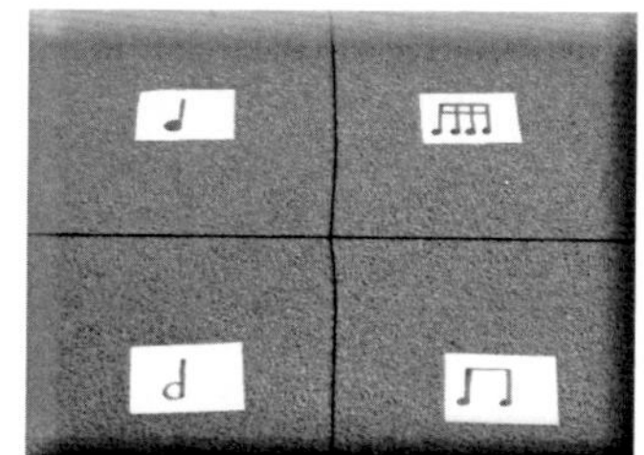

Figure 1

- Have students identify the rhythm of words or names. Create word chains and layered ostinatos by having students name food items, amusement park rides, or other lists of related words (peanuts, popcorn, cotton candy).

- Use manipulatives (rhythm sticks or popsicle sticks) to write rhythms.

- Rhythmic Echo Canons: The teacher demonstrates a four-beat rhythmic pattern. While students echo that pattern, the teacher gives another.

- Rhythm Boxes: Give students a paper with four boxes representing four beats (Fig. 2). Hand out some rhythmic note value flash cards. The flash cards should be the size of the equivalent number of boxes on the paper (Fig. 3). Use these cards for composition or dictation.

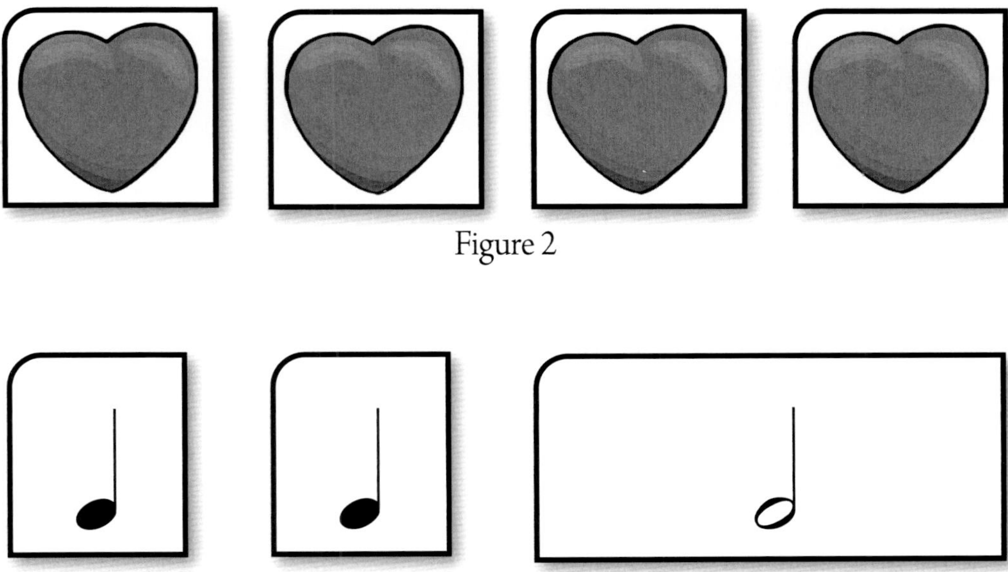

Figure 2

Figure 3

- Rhythmic Value Board Game: Make a board game with spaces lined up in a curvy road formation leading from the beginning to an ending square. Use small wooden dice with rhythms written on the dice and beans or beads as game pieces. Students move the number of spaces to coordinate with the rhythmic value they rolled.
- To make the board game more advanced, add more musical concepts.
    - » Make shortcuts entitled Accelerando Avenue or Presto Parkway.
    - » Make fermata spaces where a student waits a turn before continuing.
    - » Make repeat signs on two different spots.
    - » Put a *D.C. al fine* on the dice indicating students go back to the start.
- Have students say, move, or play instruments to repetitive phrases in a children's book.
- Rhythmic Math: Give students rhythm problems to solve.

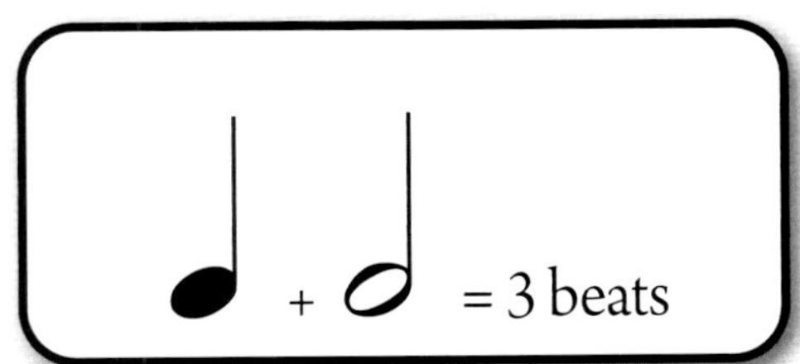

Meter

Movement for Strong and Weak Beats
- Tennis Ball Patterns: Bounce tennis balls on the strong beats; hold or juggle them between the left and right hands on the weak beats.
- Add singing games or traditional jump rope rhymes to the tennis ball patterns.
- Stomp on strong beats and clap quietly on weak beats as the teacher improvises on an

instrument of choice. Then clap the strong beat and tiptoe the weak beats.

- Pass a ball in one direction, but change directions each time a new meter is heard.
- Create hand jives individually or with partners to show 4/4 and 3/4 meter. A 4/4 pattern could be stomp, pat, snap right, snap left. A 3/4 pattern could be pat, clap, snap.

Changes in Meter

- Pass a Yarn Ball: Have the class sit in a circle and pass the ball until they hear the meter change. Try passing two or three balls at a time.
- Listen to music and have the class congregate into groups of students equalling the meter. (If the song is in 3/4, students get into groups of three.)
- Walk in shared space, changing direction each time a new meter is heard.
- In a circle, give each student a tennis ball. Ask students to make up a pattern allowing them to pass the ball in the meter given, but change direction when the meter changes. The ball-passing pattern should reflect the strong beats of the meters.

Bar Lines and Measures

- Draw football goal posts and explain how a field goal is scored when the ball is kicked <u>through</u> the goal (Fig. 1). The teacher relates this to music by explaining bar lines are like goal posts and the rhythms inside the bar lines make up a measure. Count the beat values in each measure. Erase part of the goal posts to transform them into a measure (Fig. 2). Rename the field goal a measure and the goal posts bar lines.

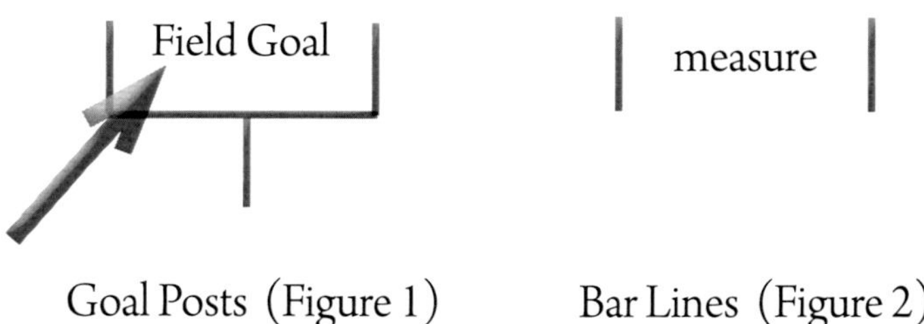

Goal Posts (Figure 1)   Bar Lines (Figure 2)

Time Signatures

Explain how time signatures tell the number of beats in each measure. Demonstrate how different combinations of rhythms complete a measure in certain time signatures. Help students create rhythms to complete a measure in various time signatures.

- Fill in the Measure:
  - » Students choose a card or roll a die with rhythms on it. They decide if their roll fits into a given measure.
  - » Each student in turn rolls the dice and determines whether or not their note value can fit in the measure according to the time signature.
  - » When a measure is completed, begin a new measure to continue the game.
- Have students compose rhythmic ostinatos in specific meters.

- Look for Melodic Direction Listening Maps in your district-adopted textbooks or make them with pictures, dots, and/or lines.
- Make Melodic Direction cards for a song and have students discover the order of the cards.

- Use a parachute to have students respond to melodies going up or down in recorded or sung songs.
- Use tennis balls to respond to high and low sounds. If students hear a high sound, they throw the ball in the air, but if the sound is low, they drop the ball.
- Use books or rhymes which highlight melodic direction (*Hickory, Dickory, Dock*).
- Create a melody to sing or play repetitive phrases from children's books.

Use movement to determine whether students hear melody and/or harmony. Students walk only when they hear the melody. When harmony is present, students freeze. Use a musical recording or teacher improvisation on piano or an Orff instrument.

Identifying/ Playing Chord Changes
- Change directions when chords change.
- Create frozen shapes individually or in groups and change between these shapes as the music requires.
- Use colored squares to indicate chord changes.

> » Place these colored cards on the words of the song or on the score. Add the harmonic rhythm of the accompaniment to the colored squares.
> » After students have some experiences using colors, Roman numerals or chord letters could be added.

- Respond to chord changes using body percussion. Clap the I chord and stomp the V chord. If you have a IV chord, use patschen.
- Create frozen shapes for each chord; students switch shapes as the harmony changes.
- Colored Chords: Have half the class play the red chords and half play the blue. Switch parts.
- Advanced students perform all of the chords in a song through simple or alternating/broken borduns. Syncopated rhythms may also be added to the bordun patterns.

- Perform partner songs.   You can find partner songs in **Grab a Partner** and **Grab Another Partner** (Albrecht and Althouse).
- Perform rounds.
- Perform vocal ostinatos.

Use simplified vocal exercises much like warm-ups. Use vowel sounds or ask students to speak rhymes like *Jack and Jill* with varied pitch and timbre.

 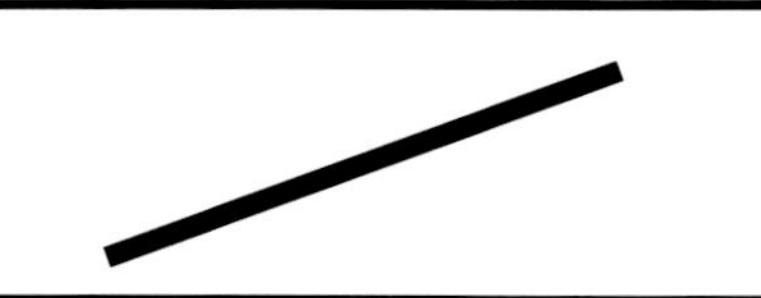 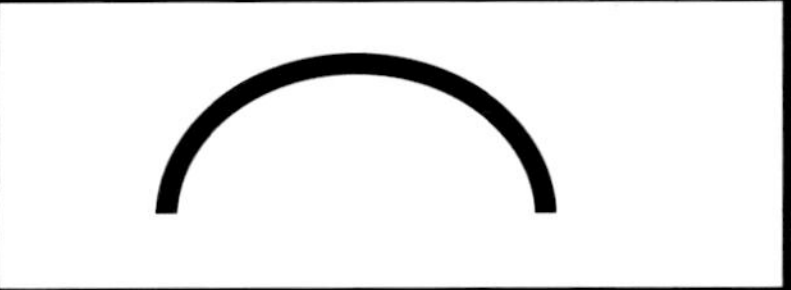

- Many books help students explore their voices, such as **Doggies** (Boynton), which tells about different dogs with different barks.

- Use PVC phones. If a student is having difficulty matching pitch, connect two PVC elbow

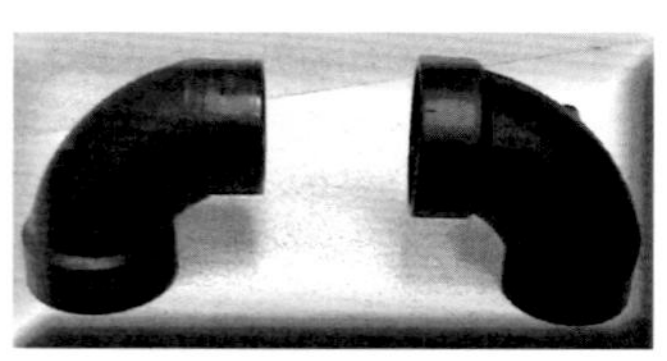  

  joints (purchased from a local hardware store). When connected, they look like a phone. The student puts one end near their ear and the other near their mouth. They will be able to hear their own singing.
  - » Turn one side of the phone around. Let the student not matching pitch put one end by their ear and listen to another student who is matching pitch singing into the other end.
- Have students play singing games where students sing solo, such as *Doggie, Doggie, Where's The Bone* or *Button You Must Wander*. Games work well because students are not self-conscious about singing alone if they are having fun playing a game.
- Use props.
  - » Students self-conscious about singing solo can use a pretend microphone to help them overcome shyness.
  - » Hand students small objects as they are walking in the door. When they are seated, sing, *"Who has the blue square?"* The student answers, *"I have the blue square,"* matching the same pitches. Use small animal erasers, pieces of paper with rhythms printed on them, or colored scarves.

Tempo

- Act out poems, songs, and stories which lend themselves to tempo variations.
- Ask students to respond individually in movement to tempos and tempo changes in a teacher improvisation or recorded music selection.
- Help students choose movements to represent each tempo marking and respond as a group to teacher improvisation or recorded music.
- Arrange familiar songs. Students determine or set the tempo or tempo changes. This could be done by writing the tempo markings on the board.
- Student leaders indicate the tempo on a drum during an eight-beat introduction.
- Have the class help make two arrangements of a song at different tempos, record both, and compare.
- Make Listening Maps. (You can find a full-color listening map in the Supplemental Materials.)
  - » Make a listening map and have students keep track of the beat throughout a song. A good listening example with an accelerando is *In the Hall of the Mountain King* (Grieg). Make a map with16 footsteps to follow through a mountain. Students use popsicle sticks to point to each footstep representing a beat. The students follow the 16-beat pattern as it repeats and speeds up.
  - » Use pictures to represent the tempo changes such as rabbits and turtles.
- Perform steady beat and singing games adding an accelerando.
- Perform hand jives adding an accelerando. Here is an example:

Twist and Twirl

Jane Barbe

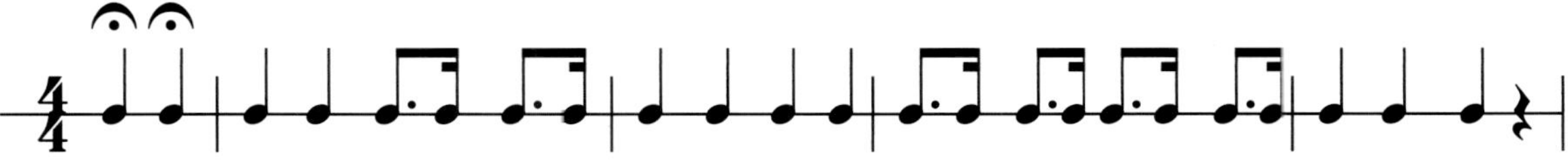

Hand Jive Pattern

P = Pat.
CL = Clap own hands.
RT = Tap your right hand to your partner's right hand.
LFT = Tap your left hand to your partner's left hand.
T = Tap both of your palms with your partner's palms.

Formation: Partners in scattered formation around the room.

Process
- Teach hand jive pattern to students silently; point to self and do a motion; point to students to repeat; add one motion at a time. (Students are echoing individually at this point, not with partners.)
- State, *"I am going to add something to my motions. Please tell us what I added and where I added it."*
- Silently perform the motions; elicit the answer from students.
- From this point on, the teacher holds up one finger when adding a movement, silently performs the motions, and points to students to repeat.
- Continue these silent directions until the entire pattern is proficient (pat, clap, right, clap, left, clap, together).
- Students choose partners and practice the hand jive.
- State, *"I will have you start the hand jive, and when you are consistent, I will begin saying a rhyme. Please continue the hand jive until the rhyme ends."*
- Teach rhyme phrase by phrase.
- Perform the hand jive and rhyme simultaneously.
- Students choose partners and work on the hand jive together and then with the rhyme.
- Add a transition which allows students to switch partners.

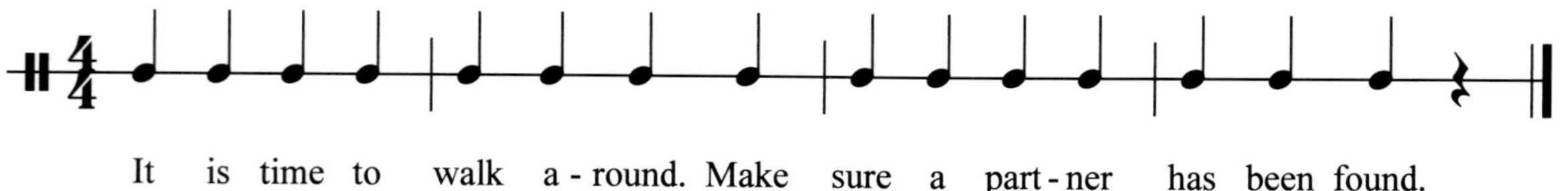

Extension
- Groups of two partners join with another partner set to create teams of four. Each partner set stands across from the other, forming a diamond.
- The group of four decides which partner set will perform the hand jive higher and which will perform it lower to avoid collisions. The "together" motions are now performed with all four students tapping their hands with their neighbors to the side. When the students are proficient in groups of four, consider having the partner sets switch who is moving higher or lower in the middle of the song (at the second pat). If the transition is utilized, have each partner set move together to find another set.

Dynamics

- Choose big movements (raise arms high or spread legs and arms) for loud and small movements (curl up in a ball) for soft.
- Hide an object and have students play hot/cold with loud/soft, using instruments rather than voices.
- Have the class arrange a song with dynamic changes.
- Arrange two songs using different dynamics, record them, and analyze the similarities and differences.
- Read poems or books which indicate dynamic changes and respond in movement or with instruments.
- Create wind storms, rain storms, and/or thunder storms using body instruments, drums, or classroom percussion instruments. Build the storms and have them subside.
- Use books which lend themselves to crescendos and decrescendos such as ***Thump, Thump, Rat-a-Tat-Tat*** (Baer).

Tonality

Major and Minor

- Use descriptive words to represent the sound of major and minor.
- Walk; change directions when you hear changes between major and minor.
- Create movements for each tonality.
- Identify when tonality changes.
- Listen to a recording; have students map the tonality with colored paper squares.

Scales/Half Steps and Whole Steps

- Play a game where students work their way up a paper piano moving by whole steps and half steps. Flip a penny for the moves (heads = whole step; tails = half step).
- Teach a scale as a pattern of whole and half steps.

Recorder Playing

- Use songs and rhymes to reinforce fingerings. The rhymes or songs say the note name and the fingers placed on the recorder produce that note.

1 Plus Thumb

Jane Barbe

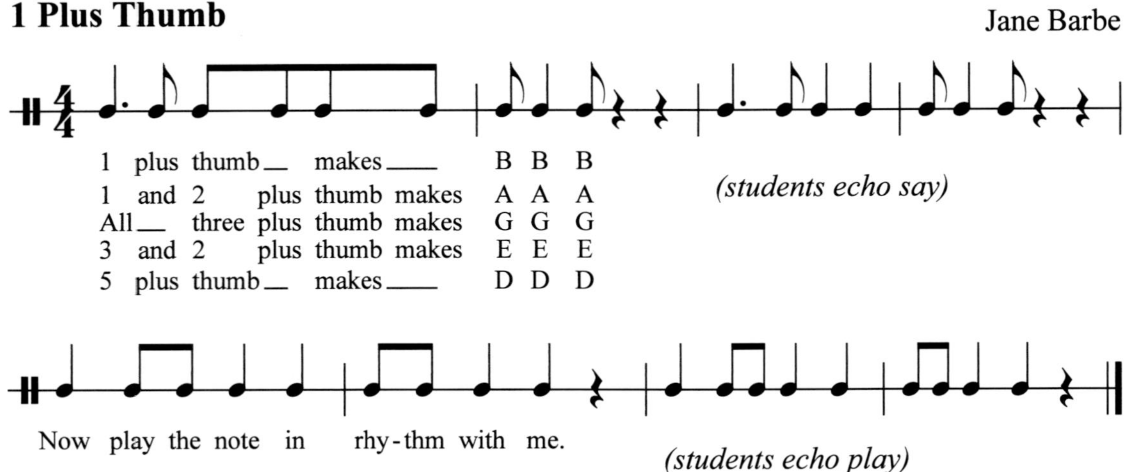

- Use body percussion to teach the pattern of a song (snap B's, clap A's and patsch G's).
- Echo Patterns (for fingerings): Use a chart of letter names on the board to point out a short series of notes. Students respond by playing the series of notes on recorder with the correct fingerings.
- Echo Patterns (for reading): Use a chart with notes on the staff instead of letter names.

B
A
G
E
D

- Recorder Relay: Students in a line play an already learned song one note at a time down the line.
- Use this process for students when learning a song on their own or guided by a teacher.
    » Read the rhythm.
    » Read the note names; say them in rhythm.
    » Learn and practice the fingerings in rhythm, without actually playing the instrument.
    » Play the song.
- Create a recorder melody to a repetitive phrase from a children's book such as **Bringing the Rain to Kapiti Plain** (Aardema). Students also love to dramatize this story and/or add instrument accompaniment to the recorder melody.

Form

- Identify sections by colors.
- Identify sections by shapes.
- Identify sections by letters (ABA).

- Have students move only on a certain section.
- Create different movements for each section.
- Teach the A Section of a folk dance. Ask students to perform it when the A Section is heard. Identify the different section or B Section. Learn the dance for the B Section; put the two sections together. Discover the form of the whole piece and perform.
- Create a frozen shape for each section; change shapes as the sections change.
- Use colored streamers to highlight the form.
    » Let students make their own colored streamer on a stick.
    » Assign each streamer color to a section of the music.
    » Students group themselves by color and create a movement with their streamers during their assigned section of the music.

Timbre

- Have students react in movement to instrument sounds or families (wood = walk, metal = tiptoe, drum = hop).
- Play hide and seek. Let a student hide and play an instrument. Ask the class to identify the instrument heard by naming it verbally or holding up a picture card.
- Have students play three instruments in a row, two in the same family and one from another family. Identify the different instrument.
- Discuss instrument families and groupings by how they are played and their sound, rather than by their material.
- Identify an instrument in one family; have students go on a scavenger hunt to find the rest of the instruments in that family.
- Use literature with descriptive words and decide which instruments resemble those sounds.
- Create stories and have instruments play on certain words.
- Have students add movement to ostinatos; accompany them with voice and body instrument sounds.
- Have students create sound carpets to poems or songs.
- Have students create poems or haikus and match instruments to their sound elements.
- Use Listening Maps with pictures of instruments to help students hear specific instrument sounds in classical pieces.
- Have students react to instruments through movement. Play a recording and focus on one sound, such as the flute. Every time they hear the flute, they perform a creative movement reflecting the sound they hear.
- Have students choose instruments to represent characters or sounds in a children's book such as ***The Little Old Lady Who Was Not Afraid of Anything*** (Williams) or ***Way Out in the Desert*** (Marsh and Ward).
- Play Orff instruments on certain rhyming words in songs.

Little Miss (Muffet,) sat on her (tuffet.)

Eating her curds and (whey.)

Along came a (spider)

Who sat down (beside her)

And scared Miss Muffet (away)

◯ = drums; transfer to metallophone

⬠ = triangles; transfer to glockenspiel

▭ = woodblocks; transfer to xylophones

Sample introduction to the term "Timbre"

TEACHER: Today, we are going to learn what the word *timbre* means. You would think it would be spelled *tamber,* but the word is from the Italian language, so it is spelled *timbre.* Have you ever been in the backyard and you hear this? (Knock on the door.) How do you know where it comes from?

STUDENT: You listen for where the sound comes from.

TEACHER: What sound did you hear?

STUDENT: Someone knocking at the door.

TEACHER: How did you know it wasn't someone knocking at the window?

STUDENT: The sound would be different.

TEACHER: You are correct. The window would sound higher and lighter. So you are saying wood and glass have different timbres, OK? Has anyone figured out what *timbre* means?

STUDENT: It's the sound something makes.

TEACHER: Correct. Can we make timbre with our bodies?

STUDENT: We can snap, pat, and stomp.

TEACHER: Good. Do we have timbre in our voices? Are all our voices the same?

STUDENT: No.

TEACHER: So, you are saying everyone's voice has a different timbre?
STUDENT: Yes.
TEACHER: Today we are going to experiment with the different timbres of our percussion instruments.

Use rotation activities. Many published resources emphasize the use of interludes to rotate students efficiently and quietly in a determined number of beats. Give students eight or 16 beats to change partners or instruments before the A Section begins anew. Here's an example:

Four White Horses

Traditional Caribbean Folk Song

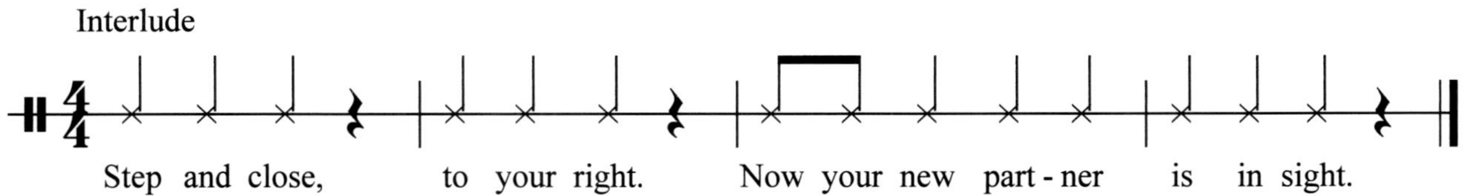

B Section Interlude Alternate Words

Instruments down and get in line to play an instrument right on time.

or

Sit up straight, there you'll wait, until it's your turn, then don't be late.

Concerts: Creating Themes and Program Planning

Each teacher has a personal style for performances depending on their type of training and educational background. Some teachers prefer musicals where students sing in groups while others highlight solo singing. This book reflects the wholistic style of Orff Schulwerk when all students learn and perform all the activities. Concerts include student instrumental accompaniment, vocal performance, and movement using interchangeable sets of students for each component.

How Do I Choose Songs or Themes for Concerts?

Concert choices present many challenges for teachers. Always choose quality material when designing your program.
- Collect pieces drawing out a common theme.
- Use a theme like space and space exploration; look for lesson books in music catalogs or search through district-adopted texts for relevant songs.
- Perform an Orff-based thematic program purchased from a music catalog which includes songs, instrument accompaniments, and movement.

How Many Songs Should I Include in a Program?

- Performances Involving Instruments, Movements, and Singing
    » When designing a program, a good rule of thumb is one song per class so you can assign the instruments, singing, and movement equally.
    » Add one song at the beginning and/or end of the program which everyone can sing with a recording or piano accompaniment.
- Vocal Performances
    » For a choir concert with no Orff instruments, prepare six to eight songs (unison songs, partner songs, rounds, and two- or three-part songs).

Who Should Perform?

- Any grade level can perform. Ask school administrators what the tradition has been in the past, or establish new ones.

Who Should Perform Together?

- In large schools with more than three classes in each grade level, consider having only one grade level perform at a time.

- With less than three classes per grade level, adjoining grade levels can perform together (2nd and 3rd or 4th and 5th).
- Smaller schools could have a whole school program with younger students singing and performing simpler voice, instrument, or movement parts while older students perform more complex parts.

- If you have five classes performing in a concert, have class A perform the instrumental accompaniment, class B perform the movement, and classes C, D, and E perform the vocal parts.
- Rotate the classes for each song so all students sing, play instruments, and move at some point in the concert.

Set up a chart to organize the classes in a concert. Each class performs an instrument accompaniment, movement accompaniment, recorder, and drumming piece. Each class also has at least one vocal performance piece.

Fife and Drum

Class A
Orff Instruments: *Tahiya*
Drumming: *Winter Winds*
Movement: *Ashante*
Recorder: *Magdelaina*
Singing: *Aito*

Class C
Orff Instruments: *Aito*
Drumming: *Magdelaina*
Movement: *Winter Winds*
Recorder: *Tahiya*
Singing: *Ashante*

Class B
Orff Instruments: *Magdelaina*
Drumming: *Ashante*
Movement: *Tahiya*
Recorder: *Aito*
Singing: *Winter Winds*

Class D
Orff Instruments: *Ashante*
Drumming: *Aito*
Movement: *Magdelaina*
Recorder: *Winter Winds*
Singing: *Tahiya*

Consider style, tempo, and form.
- Type of piece
  - » Vocal piece with CD or piano accompaniment
  - » Speech piece highlighting rhythms (with or without unpitched instruments)
  - » Rhythm instrumental piece
  - » Barred instrumental piece
  - » Piece including layered rhythmic/instrumental ostinati
  - » Pieces including layered speech ostinati
  - » Pieces including layered vocal ostinati

» Pieces in unison

» Partner songs

» Rounds and canons

» Two- or three-part vocal pieces

- Full Performance Pieces (vocal, instrumental accompaniment, movement)

» Drumming

» Literature (Act out a story and add a song with reoccurring Orff accompaniment.)

» Canons

» Call and response

Possible Themes

- Insects
- Power of Music
- The Power of Play (Games That Teach)
- Festival of Celebration (Celebrations Around the World)
- Making Music through Literature (Stories)
- Multicultural (Native American, African, Hispanic)
- Space
- Jungle
- Circus
- Jazz
- Fife (Recorder) and Drumming
- Got A Question? We've Got the Answer (Question and Answer Pieces)

Backdrops/Props:

- Use simple backdrops to focus on the music or elaborate ones to enhance the performance. Elaborate backdrops are often needed when recreating a story or performing a musical. In this case, ask for parent volunteers who will help if you just ask. Often the art teacher will collaborate as well.

Tip: Why Concerts?

Concerts, an important part of the music curriculum, allow students to gain confidence and show the results of what they have learned in class. This type of accountability is a valuable part of education.

Concerts are good public relations for the school and build relationships with the community at large as well as parents and patrons.

Concerts are a great deal of work, yet with careful advance planning, they will run smoothly and be rewarding for both teacher and students.

Concerts: Preparing Students and Rehearsals

Preparing students for a performance often takes five to eight weeks, depending on how often each class meets and whether songs, instrumental pieces, or movement activities students already know are selected.

Teach every class all of the instrument and singing parts. Because classes will not practice together until two weeks before the concert, knowing all the parts will help students work as an ensemble at concert time. When you assign parts, make a point of teaching and/or demonstrating what other classes do in the same song.

Notice which class easily learns the instrument and singing parts during class. Assign the parts to each class based on their classroom performance.

Teach students how to transition between songs. If students are unsure what song comes next, what their part is, or where they are supposed to move, they cannot concentrate on the music. Make transitions second nature for students.   During concerts, students can be in one of three places during any given song:

- the stage (movement, dance)
- the stairs and/or risers (singing and speaking)
- the Orff and unpitched instruments

Use a process to ensure quiet and efficient transitions.

Two Weeks Before the Concert

- Take students to the performing area to show them the location of each station (instruments, risers, and stage). If going to the area is not possible, draw students a map of the area.
- Display the order of the pieces by number. Ask each class where they will be for each piece in the order. Ask, *"Where will you be for #1? Where will you be for #2?"*
- Break it down for students. If they are on the risers for the majority of the pieces, ask them on which pieces they have to remember to move.

One Week Before the Concert
* Take students to the performance area to walk through the pieces in order (risers, stage, instruments). If this is not possible, use paper on the floor in your room to designate the areas in the performance area and have students walk the mock setup in the order of the concert.

This rehearsal process pays off in the quality of the student performance. You will receive as many compliments on the smooth transitions as the music performances.

TIP

Technology Rehearsal Preparation
Today's technology can change the way we prepare for rehearsals. Most computers now have the capability to record sound and store it as .mp3 or .wav files. Your computer may already contain such a program. If not, free software is available.
* *Record each class performing their part of a song.*
* *Have the other classes perform their part with the recording.*
* *Use technology during full rehearsals.*
  * *Record the students' performance of a piece, a particular part of a piece, or their transition between pieces.*
  * *Play the recording for the students; have them analyze their performance.*
  * *Record again; mark the improvements and any revisions still needed.*

How Many Massed Rehearsals Will I Need?

Plan for two or three one-hour rehearsals in the period before the concert and a half-hour final rehearsal in the days before the concert.

Scheduling Rehearsals

Consider the possibilities when scheduling rehearsals.
* Ask for a substitute teacher to cover classes during rehearsals and performances.
* Schedule rehearsals during the music time of the grade levels performing in the concert.
* Reschedule non-performing classes outside the time block designated for rehearsals.
* Have a non-performing class observe the rehearsal during their regular class time. (Let students practice or learn proper audience behavior. You might even have the observing class watch for and comment on certain aspects of the rehearsal.)

When picking concert dates and times, directly and immediately contact all teachers involved (including special area teachers, special education teachers, classroom teachers), the principal, and the school secretary. Make a rehearsal schedule available to the person responsible for building use and calendar keeping. Schedule the rehearsal room. Check testing and field trip schedules with classroom teachers. Give everyone a day or two to respond before finalizing the schedule.

<table>
<tr><td>TIP</td></tr>
<tr><td>Concert dates and times should be set months in advance to avoid conflicts regarding the use of space, field trips, testing, or other assemblies.</td></tr>
</table>

Main Goal of Rehearsals

With few opportunities to combine classes for practice, focus rehearsals to show students what to do for each song and how songs fit together as a puzzle. This analogy draws their attention to how parts fit together. Ask questions such as:

- How many beats of introduction do you hear from the instruments before I cue you to sing?
- Who plays when you perform your movement on stage?
- Does your instrument part line up with any other part?

Rehearsal Format

Initial Rehearsal

- Establish behavior guidelines and consequences.
- Establish clear directions for moving to each area.
  - » Tape separate up and down arrows or lines on the stairs to the stage. The arrows/lines maintain order as one class moves onto the stage while another exits. Students should walk single file with their feet on the arrows as they enter and exit the stage.
  - » Mark by arrows or lines which side students enter and exit the instrument area in front of the stage.
  - » Tell students how to file on and off the risers.
- Have students move to each station in the order of the program. All classes moving for each piece should move at the same time. Do this without music, silently, upon the teacher's signal. Say, *"Piece #1. Piece #2."*
- Start with Piece #1 with each class showing the others their part.
- Perform Piece #1 with all parts combined.
- Refine any rough sections.
- Move on to the other pieces in order until the end of the rehearsal time.
- Throughout the rehearsal, record these performances and analyze them as a group.
- End the rehearsal with positive feedback, an overview of the next rehearsal (including areas for refining), and a final positive comment.

Subsequent Rehearsals
- Have students move to each station in the order of the concert and begin each piece.
- Begin run-throughs on the pieces not rehearsed during the first rehearsal.
- Reserve time to focus on the beginning and end of each piece to ensure students begin and end together, which requires students understand your conducting patterns and the form for each piece.
- Run the entire performance without interruption.
- Go back and work on the most difficult pieces.
- End the rehearsal with positive feedback, an overview of the next rehearsal (including areas for refining), and a final positive comment.

Final Rehearsal/Dress Rehearsal
- Run through the concert without interruption.
- Discuss areas of concern and provide conducting solutions.
- End with positive encouragement. Say, *"I know you will see many people in the audience, but remember it's you and me up there, just like in rehearsals. I have confidence in you. Remember to listen to each other and watch me, and you will be awesome!"*

Concert Set-Up
- Concert set-up possibilities are endless. This book focuses on set-ups for Orff-based programs which include instrument accompaniment, movement, and vocal performance.
- Most importantly in any set up, keep sight lines open for parents to view all aspects of the performance.

Many schools have permanent stairs in front of the stage while others have portable risers. The diagram below involves placing students on permanent stairs with Orff instruments on the floor in front.

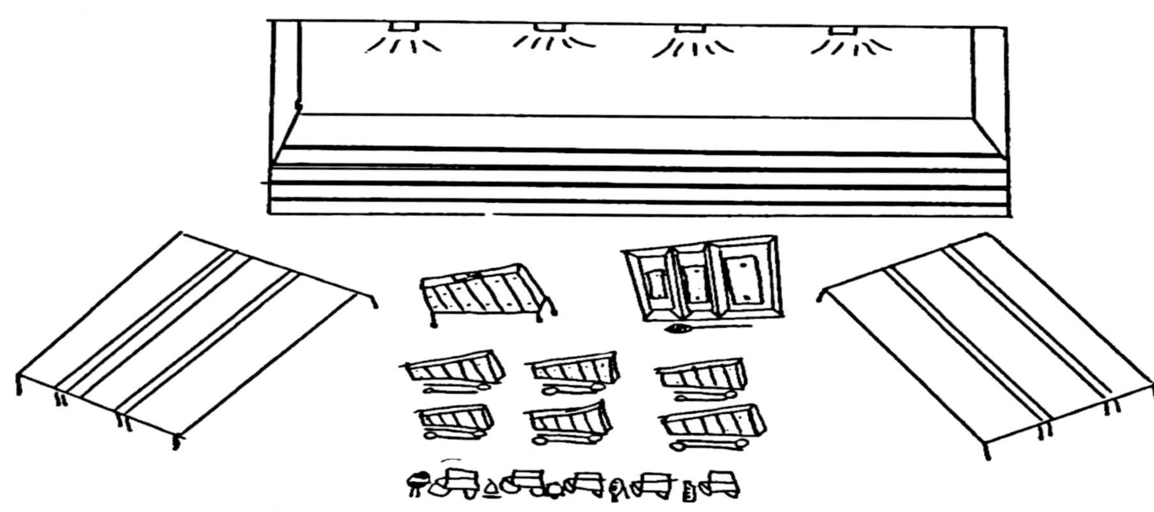

- In this set-up, students sit during pieces where movement occurs on stage.
- Place instruments on tables or desks.
- Place unpitched instruments on chairs next to or in front of barred instruments. The chairs give students designated places to sit and keep the instruments orderly throughout the concert. Several unpitched instruments can be placed underneath each chair to reduce the number of chairs in the set-up. Use enough chairs for the number of unpitched instruments in the largest concert piece.
- Place instruments on stage if movement is not involved in the concert.
- Students singing in this set up will be heard, but not seen.
- Place risers to the side to allow students to sit on certain pieces or stand to perform movement on others. Portable risers work well to open up the sight lines for parents.
- Place instruments on desks or tables in front of the stage. Place unpitched instruments under chairs to the front or side of barred instruments.
- Utilize the stage for movement.
- When movement is not involved, place risers and/or instruments on stage.

Supervision During the Concert

Ask classroom teachers or parent volunteers to help with the arrival and exit of students. An administrator will attend evening events and can welcome parents and friends and introduce the concert.

Where Do Students Meet for Evening Performances?

Students can gather in the music room or in their homerooms. Because they will be very excited, they should know where to go and what is expected of them in advance. Having students meet in the music room allows them to gather recorders if needed, but meeting there puts many people in a small space. Having students meet in classrooms may be a better option if classroom teachers are prepared in advance. Classroom teachers could distribute labelled recorders.

Dismissing Students After Evening Performances

Have students go to the music room where a classroom teacher or parent volunteer releases them to their parents. Give each teacher or volunteer a sign-out sheet. An administrator at every after-school function will ensure each child gets home safely.

How Do I Introduce the Concert?

Welcome parents and introduce yourself. Keep remarks to a minimum, explain what students will be playing, and present the group. Say,

Hello, and welcome to our program. Tonight we will present a concert on (theme). Students have been working very hard to learn to play as an ensemble. This requires listening and understanding how each part of the song fits together. The concepts taught during this program are listed in your program. Now I would like to present students of the third grade.

Having students announce each song can be very effective. Many teachers choose their best readers while others choose students who would do a good job and could use an extra boost in confidence. Speech parts could be memorized or read from notes. Have students represented from each class and have them practice during the rehearsals.

Unless you have a separate gym or auditorium, performances will probably be in a multi-purpose room, which may also be the physical education classroom. If so, work with the physical education staff to schedule rehearsals and concert dates. Offer the music room to physical education teachers if music classes are not meeting during the rehearsals and performances.

Notifying Parents About Behavior

Most teachers dread having to contact parents, yet the process can be a positive and effective way of building teamwork between the student, parents, and teacher.   Initiate such conversation early rather than contacting parents telling them their child has been misbehaving for weeks.

- Prepare before calling. Some teachers even write out what they are going to say beforehand.
- Let parents know you are concerned about their child's behavior and about how their child can be helped to have a positive experience in your class.
- State the facts unemotionally.
- Inform parents of strategies used to prevent and/or stop the behavior.
- Let parents know strategies to help the student make better choices.
- Focus the conversation on teamwork between the parent, the teacher, and the student.
- Remember the parent can often give a great deal of information to help in understanding their child.
- Avoid verbalizing personal reactions to the incident or drawing conclusions.
- Avoid violating school confidentiality agreements by mentioning the names of other students involved.

Sample Narrative

Whether by phone or by email, always introduce yourself, state what occurred and the attempted interventions, and offer strategies which might be tried.

Hello, may I speak to a parent of ______________? This is Jane Barbe, the music educator at ______________ school. I am calling in regards to Jamie's behavior in music class today. She was having a difficult time making good choices in terms of talking This was the second class I had to talk to Jamie about her behavior. The first day I gave her the chance to fix it on her own. Since this was the second class, I wanted to let you know. When I talked to Jamie, I let her know I noticed she was talking in the beginning of class and asked her what she thought she needed to do to make better choices. She said she needed to move away from the student she was talking to. After moving, she began talking to another student. I asked her if she thought going to time out if her talking continued was reasonable as a consequence of not following expectations, and she said it was. She did end up going to time out, and I thought you would want to know.

At this point, let the parent talk. Offer strategies you want to try to help the student make better choices. The parent might agree or offer something they think would work better. At the end of the conversation, thank them for the information they gave about their child and let them know you will be in touch if further problems occur.

<table>
<tr><td>TIP</td></tr>
<tr><td>Always take notes during parent phone calls. Also print out all emails and keep these items in a section of your planning binder or other place where you keep confidential information.</td></tr>
</table>

To the Parent/Guardian of _________________________________ Date _____________

Your child had some difficulties making appropriate choices at school today.

The problem area(s) are marked below:

- talking instead of working/listening   _______
- following directions   _______
- obscene/lewd language/gestures   _______
- defiance/lack of cooperation   _______
- daydreaming/inattentive   _______
- inappropriate use of hands/feet   _______
- other   _______

The following actions were taken to help the student make better choices:

- reminders/warnings   _______
- discussion of expectations   _______
- reflective time-out: in our classroom   _______
  - in another classroom   _______

Loss of privileges (if any):

- materials/ instruments   _______
- alternative assignment   _______
- alternative setting   _______
- classroom recess   _______
- lunch recess   _______
- other   _______

Please sign and return this note to me tomorrow. Your support and feedback regarding this information is appreciated.

Thank you,
J. Barbe
Music Specialist

Available as a text file in Supplemental Materials

I have read this Classroom Behavior Notification and discussed today's difficulty with my child.

Parent/Guardian Signature_____________________________Date__________________

Lesson Ideas for Substitute Teachers

Substitute lesson plans (created in advance) must be engaging and musically relevant, yet easy for the substitute teacher to present. Many substitutes are reluctant to accept music positions if lessons are too difficult. With engaging and well organized lessons, substitutes will accept the position without reservation.

Put all substitute lessons in a designated container. Label each lesson with a number or letter. When you leave instructions, simply state the grade level and the lesson number or letter of the lesson for the class period. Keep the container in a permanent place easily spotted by the substitute.

- Use a quality video and list focus questions for the substitute to put on the board. Choose a video about orchestra instruments, a style of music like jazz, or a popular touring movement/instrument group, or use a series video from your district-adopted text.
- Videotape yourself playing a game with students and have them play along. You have to give instructions on the video and record it for the same amount of time as the class period. When you tape the game, act as though you have a class there with you. This takes time, but will save you a great deal of headache when you need to be out unexpectedly.
- Create an audio tape of a lesson or game as above.
- Tape yourself playing piano to traditional beat proficiency games students already know.
- Tape yourself playing a melodic or rhythmic ear training game. Have students play against you and have the substitute teacher keep score. (Make sure you state on the tape what conditions allow students to earn a point.) Students want to play these forever.

If the substitute has a musical background, let them teach any game from one of these sources.

Great Singing Games for Children (Amidon)
More Great Singing Games for Children (Amidon)
Singing Games Children Love Volume I (Gagne)

Assessing Student Progress

- Use singing games with elementary students. Students are less inhibited to sing alone during games, especially when hidden from view or while using a prop (blow up microphone or puppet).
    - » Use singing games with hidden objects (*Doggie, Doggie, Where's Your Bone* or *Button, You Must Wander*).
    - » Use call and response songs or singing games with solo responses (even name games).
- Students of all ages like to be given objects they will later be asked about in song. Give each student a farm animal eraser, a colored paper square, or a finger puppet as they walk in the door. When students are seated, sing, *"Who has the green square?"* That student echoes the teacher's singing melodically with the words, *"I have the green square."*

- Assess beat competency and understanding of rhythm with games with a rhythmic pattern to be read, clapped, or played.

Sample Assessment Activity

- Make assessment cards for each grade-level-appropriate rhythm K-5 written on pictures of records.
- Say the rhyme:

Rockin' Rhythms, Rockin' Rhythms,
That's the game.
Rockin' Rhythms, Rockin' Rhythms,
When I say your name.

- Students read, clap, or play the rhythm on an instrument depending on what being assessed. *I Hope* from **Grade 1 Game Plan** (Kriske and DeLelles) shows students using assessment cards to read or play the given rhythm pattern.

Compositions

- Have older students compose rhythmic compositions or ostinatos.
    - » Have students create a four-beat ostinato using ice cream sundae toppings.
    - » Students name four one-beat toppings.
    - » Students determine the number of syllables in each word and connect it to the rhythm with the same sounds per beat (fudge = quarter note; peanut butter = sixteenth note; butterscotch = division of the sixteenth note).

Form

- Have students arrange colored cards to represent each section of a recorded song or one learned in class.
- Have students arrange cards with letters.
- Have students choose a movement or a frozen shape to perform during each section. Observe student movements to see if they change shapes accurately with the sections.
- Use these ideas with a written multiple choice activity.

Timbre

- Play games with hidden instruments. When instrument is played, students identify the instrument by picture or name.
- Use this idea with a written multiple choice activity.
- Match instruments in the same family (orchestra or classroom instruments).
- Describe sounds of instruments.

Melodic Direction

- Ask students to order bells low to high or high to low.
- Find the correct iconic representation of the melodic direction from a stack of cards. Use lines, dots, dots connected by lines, solfege signs, staircase shapes, and/or shapes from the theme of a song.
- Match the correct melodic direction card with the melody written on the staff.
- Place cards depicting the melody (iconic representations or notated on the staff) in order.

 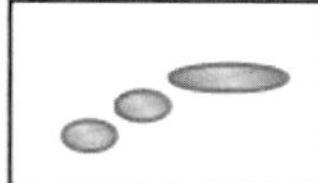 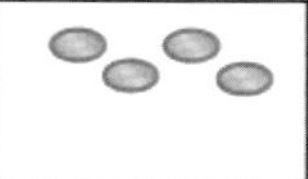 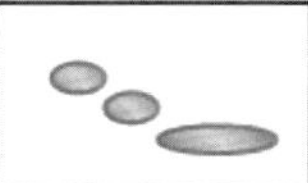

- Transcribe the melody from iconic notation.

Beat and Instrument Technique

Because beat and instrument technique are harder to assess, you need to rely on teacher observation as your primary form of assessment.

- Have students keep the beat to a recorded song with a clap, pat, stomp, or walk.
- Have students keep the beat on an instrument.
- Play beat passing games (*Banana Split*, p. 20).
- Have students perform a hand jive to a recorded song or one sung while performing. For the validity of the assessment, watch them perform the assessment with several different partners. You will be able to determine if their pulse is internal or influenced by their partner.

Recording assessments is essential for documenting each student's progress. Because every district will require written documentation, your assessments must be consistent, efficient, and recorded accurately.

Use rubrics, assessment tools which apply numbers or letters to specific language detailing exactly how the student performed. Rubrics simplify the record keeping process for assessment. Keep a simple chart for each class where you can record numbers or letters related to the rubric during class. Use the rubric below to determine a student's performance.

Demonstrate Rhythmic Competency
(Proficient, Developing, and Area of Concern are the report card terms for the district.)

Proficient	6	The student demonstrates rhythmic patterns accurately in terms of tempo and beat with sensitivity and musicality.
Proficient	5	The student demonstrates rhythmic patterns in terms of tempo and beat.
Developing	4	The student demonstrates rhythmic patterns most of the time.
Developing	3	The student demonstrates rhythmic patterns some of the time.
Area of concern	2	The student is unable to demonstrate accurate rhythmic patterns.
Area of concern	1	The student does not attempt the activity.

During the actual assessment, write down the scores for each student on the chart. If you find it difficult to record them quickly, only write down scores for students who fall below or above the benchmark for Proficient.

When entering grades at the marking period, adapt your rubric entries to the grading system required by your district. Determine which scores from the rubric fall under each report card grade. If your district uses Proficient, Developing, and Area of Concern, use 6 - 5 = Proficient, 4 - 3 = Developing, and 2 - 1 = Area of Concern. If your district uses A, B, C, D, E, and F, use 6 = A, 5 = B, 4 = C, 3 = D, 2 = E, and 1 = F.

Computer software programs efficiently record assessments and let teachers record and average grades quickly. If a software program isn't available, create your own grade book spreadsheet.

Last Week of School

During the last week of school, unwanted behaviors increase; therefore, keep students active and engaged. Get together with the physical education teacher and combine classes for organized movement, folk dancing, or review games.

You will find grade-level appropriate folk dances in *Teaching Movement and Dance: A Sequential Approach to Rhythmic Movement* (Weikart).

Great sources of musical review games are:
- *101 More Music Games for Children* (Hoenen and Storms)
- *Rhythm Baseball* (Almeida)
- *Melody Baseball* (Almeida)
- *Daffy Duck Passes the Buck* (Almeida) (trivia on instruments, vocabulary, and symbols)
- *Yosemite Sam's Music Hammer* (Almeida) (rhythm and instruments)
- *Wile E. Coyote Whammo Tap* (Almeida) (symbols and rhythm)
- *Music Proficiency Pack #2 Sneaky Snake* (Almeida)
- *Music Proficiency Pack #4 Doggone Dynamics* (Almeida)
- *Music Proficiency Pack # 7 Mood Meters* (Almeida)
- *Music Proficiency Pack #9 Style Dials* (Almeida)
- *Rhythm Bingo* (Lavendar)
- *Melody Bingo* (Lavendar)
- *Lines and Spaces Bingo* (Lavendar)
- *Instrument Bingo* (Lavendar)

Grant Writing for Instruments and Equipment

At times, you need instruments, risers, props, or other materials exceeding your budget. In these cases, write a proposal to a local merchant or to your parent organization for funds. Parent organizations often cover costs for items requested by music programs because we service the entire school population. Parent organizations want you to specify the item, description, and cost. Put as much detail as possible into these proposals; the examples provide details about the item requested, its benefit for the students involved, the merchant, and the price including tax and shipping costs. Acknowledge donations and support for your program through school newsletters and community media outlets.

Date

[SCHOOL NAME]
Street Address
City, State Zip
Phone Number
Fax Number

Available as a text file in
Supplemental Materials

Donations Coordinator Name
Store Name
Street Address
City, State, Zip
Phone Number
Fax Number

Dear Name of Store Donations Coordinator:

As the students of [SCHOOL NAME] learn music through many different modes including instruments, singing, games, movement, and dance, they often use items such as scarves, yarn balls, and tennis balls. This year students will use tennis balls to understand concepts such as pitch direction and meter (patterns of strong beats, a bounce, and weak beats, a toss). The entire population of [SCHOOL NAME] will use these tennis balls often throughout the year.

Since you are in our school neighborhood, we ask whether you would donate 30 tennis balls to our music program. In turn, we will list your company name in our concert program and school newsletter.

Thank you for your time and consideration.

Sincerely,
J. Barbe
Music Educator

Thank You!

An article for your school newsletter

I want to recognize and thank the [SCHOOL NAME] PTO for their continued support of our music program. As you know, we currently own enough recorders for all of our fourth and fifth graders to play. Past experience proves students can successfully begin playing recorder as early as third grade with benefits of this early introduction showing in fourth and fifth grades. I am excited to announce the [SCHOOL NAME] PTO recently approved a proposal to purchase 100 soprano recorders for third grade students. We will use these each year to start students playing recorders during the third quarter of the third grade.

These instruments expand the music program in innumerable ways. All students who matriculate through our school will use the recorders to understand and experience the elements of music. The recorders will also enrich musical performances.

I am excited to begin this learning adventure with the third graders and to experience the ways in which the recorders will better their musical education.

Thank you, PTO!

Sincerely,
Jane Barbe
Music Educator

Available as a text file in
Supplemental Materials

Proposal 1

Date

School Street Address
Your School Phone and Extension

[SCHOOL NAME] PTO
 Street Address
City, State Zip
School Phone Number

Dear PTO:

I am writing regarding purchasing recorders for the [SCHOOL NAME] Third Grade. These would be school-owned recorders designated for third graders to check out for the school year at no cost. The recorders would be sterilized and re-used each year. (Students always have the option of buying their own; however, the majority of students use school-owned recorders. Attached is the letter sent home to 4th and 5th grade parents.)

The recorder is an incredibly important tool at this stage of their learning. I have successfully taught the recorder to 3rd graders in the past (at other schools). Presently, the school owns only enough recorders for 4th and 5th graders. Other teachers in our district start their 3rd graders, and we would like to do the same. The benefits for students as they progress through 4th and 5th grades are endless, and the improvement of their musicianship would be well noted.

<u>Benefits and Purpose of Playing Recorders</u>
The recorder is a stepping-stone in the musical development of students. By 3rd grade, students grasp the essential concepts of music and have applied them to percussion and barred instruments. Students are ready to expand and apply their knowledge to a wind instrument and use it as a bridge between understanding musical concepts and applying several concepts simultaneously.

The recorder reinforces all of the musical concepts in the curriculum and is also essential in learning to read music on a staff. Required technique directly relates to choral singing and the playing of band and orchestra instruments. Proper breathing, proper posture, good tone, and knowledge of fingerings as related to musical notes on the staff are only a few of these related concepts.

<u>Number of Recorders Needed</u>
I base the number of recorders needed on next year's population (approximately 113). If we receive the recorders this year, we would begin our current 3rd graders in the spring. Because some 4th and 5th graders provide their own recorders, I think it would be a safe estimation to buy only 100 of them.

<u>Cost of Recorders</u>
I have contacted several companies, local and national, to determine the best price.
      [COMPANY NAME AND PHONE NUMBER]
      [BRAND NAME] Recorder (catalog number - XXXXXXX)
- » 100 recorders @ $4.25 each
- » No tax in Arizona and free shipping and handling when you buy 100 or more recorders
- » Total = $425

The next best prices ranged from $445 to $495, not including shipping.

Every student will benefit from this purchase. Thank your for your time and consideration.

Sincerely,
J. Barbe
Music Educator

Proposal 2

Date

School Street Address
Your School Phone and Extension

[SCHOOL NAME] PTO
Street Address
City, State Zip
School Phone Number

Dear PTO:

I am writing regarding purchasing a D Contra Bass Bar for the [SCHOOL NAME] students. I originally presented this proposal to the PTO in September. At that time the PTO stated they would cover the remaining cost of the Bass Bar after we held one fund-raiser. The music department earned $127.04 at our restaurant fund-raiser, and I am resubmitting this proposal for the balance needed for the Bass Bar, $207.76.

We already own three Contra Bass Bars, the notes C, F, and G, but we need to add a D Contra Bass Bar to our instrumentarium. The typical vocal range of an elementary student is in the key of D until about 4th grade, when their range expands to F and G (although many songs are written in D since it is still comfortable for students). When a song is in the key of D, students play the D (tonic note) Contra Bass Bar with a pattern to support the orchestration. Because 80% of the music students' experience is in the key of D, this instrument will enrich the musical education of all of our students, as well as our musical programs.

In an orchestration, the Contra Bass Bar emphasizes the key and pulse/beat of the music. An octave lower than the bass xylophones and metallophones, the Contra Bass Bar allows students to experience a full instrumentation and hear/feel the pulse and tonality of the music. This instrument will be used to teach and reinforce all musical concepts, particularly instrument technique, harmony, texture, and meter. This Contra Bass sound is essential to achieving a full instrumentation, and the instrument will be used by all students K-5 every day of the school year.

Due to their proper usage (and size), Contra Bass Bars are sold one note at a time. I have contacted several local and national music companies to find the best price. The price of one D Contra Bass Bar ranges from $310 to $560, not including shipping (almost my entire budget for the year). The attached page contains the catalog page with a picture and the description of the item.

       [MUSIC COMPANY NAME AND PHONE NUMBER]
       Rosewood bars (catalog number - XXXXXXX pitch = d)
- » $310
- » No tax in Arizona
- » Shipping = $24.80
- » Total = $ 334.80

Thank you for your time and consideration.

Available as a text file in
Supplemental Materials

Sincerely,

J. Barbe
Music Educator

Proposal 3

Date

School Street Address
City, State Zip
Your Contact Number

[SCHOOL NAME] PTO
School Street Address
City, State Zip
School Phone Number

Dear PTO:

I am writing regarding purchasing an A Contra Bass Bar and an Alto Xylophone for the [SCHOOL NAME] Students. When [SCHOOL NAME] first opened, the music room was provided with a basic set of instruments. I have added to this collection each year for the past six years from the music budget, yet certain instruments, used every day in music classes K - 5, are too expensive to buy from the music budget. A typical elementary music class ranges from 25 to 28 students. We now have eight Orff instruments. If two students share each instrument, 16 students can play. Currently, for the entire class to play together as they do in concerts, students rotate between the Orff instruments and sets of bells. Adding an A Contra Bass Bar and an Alto Xylophone would open up four more spots for students to play on the Orff instruments. Over time, I would like to add to the instrumentation enough for each student to have their own instrument.

When playing an orchestration, the Contra Bass Bar is used to emphasize the key of the music and the pulse/beat. Therefore, if the song were in the key of D, students would play the D (tonic note) and the A Contra Bass Bar in an alternating pattern. The Contra Bass sound is essential to achieving a full instrumentation and will be used by all students K-5, practically every day of the school year. We do own a few Contra Bass bars; however, they are the notes F, C, and G. The typical vocal range of an elementary student is in the key of D until 4th grade when their range expands to F and G (although many songs are written in D since it is still comfortable for students). An octave lower than the bass xylophones and metallophones, the Contra Bass bar allows students to experience a fuller, richer instrumentation and hear/feel the pulse and tonality of the music.

Due to their size, Contra Bass bars are sold one note at a time. I have contacted several local and national music companies to find the best price. The price of one D Contra Bass Bar ranges from $310 to $560, almost my entire budget for the year. The best price came from [COMPANY NAME AND PHONE NUMBER]. The next best prices ranged from $390-560, not including shipping.

> Rosewood Bars (Catalog # XXXXXX Pitch = A)
>> » Price = $310
>> » No tax in Arizona

Xylophones (wooden barred instruments) typically play the melody and/or complicated rhythmic parts. They have a distinct sound, unlike metal instruments which play long sustained sounds. In our instrument collection, xylophones are far outweighed by metal instruments (14 to 3). To balance the ensemble sound, more xylophones are needed. The lowest price also comes from [COMPANY NAME AND PHONE NUMBER].

> Alto Xylophone (Catalog # XXXXXXX)
>> » Price = $450
>> » No tax in Arizona

The total and shipping for both instruments would be as follows:
>> » Subtotal = $760
>> » Shipping for both instruments = $33.25
>> » Total = $793.25

These instruments will be used to teach and reinforce all musical concepts, particularly, instrument technique, harmony, texture, and meter and will enrich our musical programs. The attached pages contains the catalog page with pictures and descriptions of the items.

Thank you for your time and consideration.

Sincerely,

J. Barbe
Music Educator

Establishing a Choir, Mallet, or Drumming Group

You may want to establish a vocal or instrumental performance group if your school does not have one included in the schedule. Consult with your administrator before starting such a group and consider these issues. Your administrator will be able help you answer many of these questions.

> - How will you describe your choir?
> - What are the benefits of being in choir?
> - Will you have a behavior policy?
> - Is participation in the group free?
> - Do students have to audition?
> - Which grades will you include?
> - Will you have an attendance policy?
> - When could you hold rehearsals (recess, before, or after school)?
> - When will your choir rehearse (days/times)?
> - Will the choir meet all year or for so many quarters?
> - How will you inform parents of days where there will be no choir?
> - How will you inform parents if choir rehearsal is cancelled one day?
> - How will students get home?
> - What dismissal procedures will you have?
> - Will you follow current school parent pick-up procedures?
> - Can you arrange for a bus?
> - Does your district have policies about students walking or riding their bikes home after school hours?
> - How will you provide your contact information to parents?
> - Who will parents contact if their child does not show up at home after choir?
> - How will you attain student information: teacher, grade, contact numbers, emergency contact number?

What is choir?

Choir is an OPTIONAL, free, vocal group open to any 4th and 5th graders willing to participate and attend after-school rehearsals on Tuesdays.

What are the benefits of being in a choir?

Choir is an exciting opportunity for students who love to sing and want to learn more about singing in a group ensemble. It also teaches valuable lifetime skills: self-discipline, group cooperation, self-esteem, understanding teamwork, developing a sense of persistence, and performance confidence.

When is choir?
TUESDAYS   3:05-4:05 PM

Schedule:	January 16
November 14 - First Choir Practice	January 23
November 28	January 30
December 5	February 6
December 12	February 13
January 9	CONCERT: THURSDAY, FEBRUARY 15 @
NOTE: No Practice: Nov. 23 and Dec. 19	7:30

Choir Cancellation: If choir is cancelled on a Tuesday, the directors will call the numbers given on student information sheets until they contact a parent and/or emergency contact.

Performance: February 15, 2007 @ 7:30 PM

Transportation: If needed, district school buses can transport students home after choir.

Dismissal Procedures:

Parent Pick-Up: The director will escort students to the parent pick-up area in the front of the school. The procedures will be the same as during regular school hours.

Early Pick-Up: Please enter through the office doors, PICK UP A VISITOR'S PASS, and proceed to the music room (M102) to pick up your child. Due to safety procedures, we will not dismiss a student early without a parent picking them up from the music room.

Bus Riders and After-School Care Students: The director will escort students to the bus or kid zone area and stay with them until they are all on their way home. Walkers and Bike Riders <u>MUST</u> send in a letter from a parent indicating they may walk or ride their bike home alone after school hours.

Do you have a Behavior Policy? Yes! It is in the Choir Contract.

Do you have an Absence Policy? Yes! It is in the Choir Contract.

Director: Ms. J. Barbe (555-5555)

EMERGENCY INFORMATION

1. Child's Full Name____

                (Please print clearly)

2. Homeroom Teacher____

3. Parent Contact Numbers <u>between 3:05 - 4:05 PM</u>

       Parent Contact Number 1. (____) ____-______________

       Parent Contact Number 2. (____) ____-______________

       <u>EMERGENCY CONTACT (other than a parent)</u> (____) ____-______________

TRANSPORTATION: (Please check one)

______Parent Pick-up: School dismissal procedures will be followed.

______Bike or Walker: Students must have written permission from a parent stating their child may walk or ride their bike home alone after school hours.

______Bus: Below are the only stops the bus makes after school. (List the bus stops available for after school programs. Your district will be able to tell you the information on bus stops.) Please circle the stop where you want your child to get off the bus after choir.)

Both pages available as a text files in Supplemental Materials

Behavior Policy

Choir is a fun and educational experience. For the benefit of the group as a whole, and due to the limited number of rehearsals, we require certain behavior from each student according to the six pillars of character. All school rules and behavioral expectations apply to after-school activities.

Specific examples of model behavior include:

- No talking.
- Listen to and follow directions.
- Stand/sit appropriately (without lying down).
- Be on time.
- Carry out dismissal procedures in an orderly manner.
- Respect all members of the choir.
- Respect the director.

Procedures for Parent Notification

- Each time a student is disruptive during choir, a warning card will be given.
- After two cards in one choir rehearsal, the student will be given a parent letter to be signed and returned by the following choir rehearsal.
- If a second letter must be sent home, your child will be withdrawn from choir rehearsals and the choir performance.

Attendance Policy

Attendance is critical because of the short amount of time we have to prepare a concert. We will learn something new each practice, so each member must be present.

Procedures for Parent Notification

- A letter will be sent home after the first missed practice when the student was not marked absent on the school's attendance record. The letter indicates the student has only one more unexcused absence to remain eligible to perform in the concert.
- A second letter will be sent home after the second unexcused absence indicating the student has been withdrawn from choir.

Parent Signature ____

Student Signature ____

Resources

Aardema, Verna. ***Bringing the Rain to Kapiti Plain***. New York: Puffin Books, 1981.

Albrecht, Sally, and Jay Althouse. ***Grab a Partner: Twelve Terrific Partner Songs for Young Singers***. Van Nuys: Alfred Publishing, 2001.

---. ***Grab Another Partner: Twelve Tremendous Partner Songs for Young Singers.*** Van Nuys: Alfred Publishing, 2003.

Almeida, Artie. ***Daffy Duck Passes the Buck Assessment Game***. Van Nuys: Alfred Publishing, 2001.

---. ***Mallet Madness***. Dayton, Ohio: Heritage Music Press, 2007.

---. ***Mallet Madness Strikes Again***. Dayton, Ohio: Heritage Music Press, 2009.

---. ***Melody Baseball***. Dayton, Ohio: Heritage Music Press, 2005.

---. ***Music Proficiency Pack #2 Sneaky Snake***. Dayton, Ohio: Heritage Music Press, 2005.

---. ***Music Proficiency Pack #4 Doggone Dynamics***. Dayton, Ohio: Heritage Music Press, 2005.

---. ***Music Proficiency Pack # 7 Mood Meters***. Dayton, Ohio: Heritage Music Press, 2006.

---. ***Music Proficiency Pack #9 Style Dials***. Dayton, Ohio: Heritage Music Press, 2006.

---. ***Rhythm Baseball***. Dayton, Ohio: Heritage Music Press, 2005.

---. ***Wile E. Coyote's WHAMMO!*** Van Nuys: Alfred Publishing, 2001.

---. ***Yosemite Sam's Music Hammer Game Assessment Game***. Van Nuys: Alfred Publishing, 2001.

Amidon, Peter, and Mary Alice Amidon. ***Down in the Valley: More Singing Games for Children***. Brattleboro, Vermont: New England Dancing Masters Productions, 2000.

---. ***Jump Jim Joe: Great Singing Games for Children***. Brattleboro, Vermont: New England Dancing Masters Productions, 1991.

Baer, Gene. ***Thump Thump, Rat-a-Tat-Tat***. New York: Harper Trophy, 1989.

Boynton, Sandra. ***Doggies***. New York: Little Simon, 1984.

Brummitt, David, and Lois Choksy. ***120 Singing Games and Dances for Elementary Schools***. Englewood Cliffs: Prentice-Hall, 1987.

Funk, David, and Jim Fay. ***Teaching With Love and Logic: Taking Control of Your Classroom***. Golden, Colorado: The Love and Logic Press, 1995.

Gagne, Denise. ***Singing Games Children Love Volume 1***. Red Deer, Alberta, Canada: Themes and Variations, 1997.

---. ***Singing Games Children Love Volume 2***. Red Deer, Alberta, Canada: Themes and Variations, 1997.

Grieg, Edvard. ***In the Hall of the Mountain King (Peer Gynt Suites)***. The Philadelphia Orchestra, Eugene Ormandy. Saland Music, 2009.

Judah-Lauder, Chris. ***Fun With Boomwhackers.*** Miami: Warner Brothers Publishing, 2001.

---. ***Hand Drums on the Move.*** Bridgewater, Virginia: Beatin' Path Publications, 2004.

Hampton, Walt. ***Hot Marimba.*** Wauwatosa, Wisconsin: World Music Press, 1995.

Hoenen, Jos, and Jerry Storms. ***101 More Music Games for Children***. Alameda: Hunter House, 2001.

Jenkins, Ella. ***Play Your Instruments and Make a Pretty Sound***. Smithsonian/Folkways SF 45018. 1994.

King, Carol. ***Recorder Routes I***. Lakeland, Tennessee: Memphis Musicraft Publications, 1994.

Kriske, Jeff, and Randy DeLelles. ***Game Plan Grade 1***. Las Vegas: Kid Sounds Publications, 2005.

---. ***Game Plan Grade 3***. Las Vegas: Kid Sounds Publications, 2007.

Lavendar, Cheryl. ***Lines and Spaces Bingo***. Milwaukee: Hal Leonard Corporation, 1996.

---. ***Melody Bingo.*** Milwaukee: Hal Leonard Corporation, 1990.

---. ***Rhythm Bingo.*** Milwaukee: Hal Leonard Corporation, 1996.

---. ***Instrument Bingo.*** Milwaukee: Hal Leonard Corporation, 1997.

Marsh, T. J., and Jennifer Ward. ***Way Out in the Desert.*** Flagstaff: Rising Moon, 1998.

Mexico. La Raspa. Mariachis and Marimbas. Available in Supplemental Materials

Solomon, Jim. ***Conga Town.*** Miami: Warner Brothers Publishing, 1995.

---. ***D.R.U.M.*** Van Nuys: Alfred Publishing, 1998.

Weikert, Phyllis. ***Teaching Movement and Dance***: Ypsilanti: High Scope, 2006.

Williams, Linda. ***The Little Old Lady Who Was Not Afraid of Anything.*** New York: Harper Collins Children's Books, 1986.

Index